Pregnancy Guide for Men

The All-In-One Pregnancy Guide for First-Time Dads to Prepare for the First Nine Months and Beyond

Rocky Hunter

Table of Contents

Introduction

I believe that what we become depends on what our fathers teach us at odd moments, when they aren't trying to teach us. We are formed by little scraps of wisdom. –Umberto Eco

So, you've finally received the news you had been waiting for—you're going to be a *dad*. Raising a baby is no easy job, and even though society seems to think it's mainly a woman's arena, babies need their fathers to be equal partners in the process. Amidst all this, you must be feeling excited and scared simultaneously because a father's role isn't limited to caring for the mother. They have to quickly, in a period of nine months, learn how to take care of two people. You must be wondering why two? Well, your wife becomes a whole new person when she turns into a mama bear. She is your new loud roommate who has odd sleeping times, odd times of eating, and so on.

But when you have a heart full of love, nothing feels difficult. With a bit of knowledge and correct reading (you have much to learn about the female body, brother), you'll be ready to take care of the new mommy and the baby. That being said, it's entirely normal for you to feel stuck between your changing home situation and your work life. Do you feel that you're not able to pay proper attention to either of the two? Well, you're not alone. There's constant pressure on new dads to provide financially as well as emotionally for their family and this can easily make them feel unequipped for the new role.

Let me give you some brief stats about new dads in the US. Did you know that there's a rising trend in the percentage of stay-at-home dads? Yes, according to a survey in 2016, 17% of stay-at-home parents are dads compared to a mere 10% in 1989 (Livingston & Parker, 2019). Another survey that was conducted in 2017 had 76% of the adults agree on the fact that men have to go through a lot of pressure to support their families financially (Parker et al., 2017). Moreover, working fathers are under more pressure than working moms to return to their job after the birth or adoption of a child. A 2016 survey pointed out that 49% of adults agreed that employers pressure fathers to quickly return to work after a new child, while only 18% said employers put more pressure on mothers (Horowitz et al., 2017).

So, even when dads are spending time with their families, they have this feeling that they aren't doing enough. Most of the time, pregnancy is widely viewed as a mother's battle to the point that the struggles of the fathers are barely noticed even when they're being supportive of their partners. There's so much expectation weighing down on the modern dad that, with time, some become unsure of their abilities to help the mother. The woman undergoes a lot of changes during this time, starting from morning sickness to fatigue, and seeing her go through all of those things is tough. Fathers constantly feel guilty that they can't do anything to take away some of the difficulties.

Most dads aren't aware of the intricacies of pregnancy, how the baby develops inside the woman's body, the side effects of pregnancy, and what they can do to help. The internet is so full of information on pregnancy and fatherhood that it's common for you to experience sensory overload trying to grasp all that information. You're already grappling with the fact that you're about to be a father; reading it all just makes you acutely aware of how much you don't know.

On the other hand, there's another section of fathers who might have been dads before, and while they have had this experience in the past, they know in their hearts that they could have done a better job supporting their partner through those nine months of pregnancy. If you fall in this category, you might be seeing this as your second chance and want to improve your partner's experience this time around.

Being a dad for the first time is no doubt an emotional rollercoaster and having the right person to guide you in this journey is very important.

With everything said and done, remember that you still have a few months to prepare for the pregnancy's final days and gear yourself up emotionally for everything new that's about to happen in your life. Changes like these in the family dynamics aren't always easy to deal with, but this book will provide you with the resources that will make the journey easier. I would also like to bring this to your notice that sometimes it might happen that since your partner is carrying the child, you, as the father, might feel detached from the overall process. In those moments, it's even more essential for you to stay emotionally connected to your partner. You must try and involve yourself in the process in whatever capacity you can because this will boost your morale. This can be random things like buying clothes for the baby, visiting the doctor's clinic with your partner, arranging the baby's room, etc.

It is usually seen that when fathers are involved with the process of raising a child, they provide them with a sense of security which is crucial for the overall emotional development of the kid (Pediatric Associates of Franklin, 2018). Moreover, the relationship a child has with their father is what sets the bar for them for future relationships with others in their life.

In the following chapters, you'll learn more about the pregnancy process in a month-by-month breakdown right from the first month to birth and beyond. Every week in this journey is going to be different, and slowly, you'll learn to adapt to those changes.

Chapter 1:

Month 1—The Pregnancy Paradigm Progresses

Any fool can have a child. That doesn't make you a father. It's the courage to raise a child that makes you a father. –Barack Obama

I've often heard my father saying he was flying blind for most of his childhood. My grandfather wasn't the one changing my father's diapers, nor was he the one staying up nights when he cried. He even told me one day that while growing up, he never had anyone he could look up to as a role model for being an involved father, and so when it came to his turn, he learned everything about fatherhood all by himself. For him, it was also sort of instinctive—he wanted to give me everything he didn't get during his childhood years. On some subconscious level, he was making up for the shortcomings of his early days. But the idea that a father isn't just a sidekick in the pregnancy process but can take an active part in it is a relatively newer concept. In the earlier days, such talks were considered controversial, but now, society accepts them with open arms.

Evolution of the Concept of Fatherhood

Previously, the fathers in a family were only seen as the breadwinners and when the child reached a certain age, the fathers also became the disciplinarians, but rarely were they part of the nine months of pregnancy. Some of the ways in which the role of the fathers has changed over the years are:

- An increasing percentage of fathers believe in co-parenting, and several factors contribute to this change. Some of those are the absence of an extended family that lives close by, limited post-birth care in hospitals, and an increase in two-earner households.

- Did you know that nowadays, 96% of men are present during the birth of their child? (Machin, 2021).

- There's a misconception in society that only motherhood comes instinctively, whereas fathers have to learn it all. But is it true? Well, science says no, because during fatherhood, there's a drop in the levels of testosterone, causing men to become more empathetic, hence, bringing out the fatherhood qualities in them (Machin, 2021).

- Gay fathers have shown the world that men can take on the role of both a mom and a dad when need be.

- The rise in the number of fathers taking paternity leave is definitely a huge step towards equality in parenting a child.

- The bond between a father and a child has very different dynamics than the one the child builds with its mom. Irrespective of the culture, the father's connection with the child plays a very big role in its entry into the world beyond the boundaries of the family. It helps the child build the physical and mental resilience necessary to survive in this world.

- Kids have evolved to love their playtime with their dads as it releases a wave of hormones in their bodies leading up to a mutual neurochemical reward. A very good example is the rough and tumble play.

- When the child moves on to its teenage years, the bond with the father plays an even more crucial role as it helps them overcome loneliness, build self-esteem, battle anxiety, and also have an overall smooth transition from pre-school to middle school and then to high school.

- Some men suffer from perinatal depression (PND), and things get worse if their relationship with their partners isn't good.

- Last but not least, dads aren't always biological fathers—it's anyone who steps up to fill the shoes.

Changes in the Mom

Some major changes are going on inside the body of a woman when she's pregnant, and as the father of the child, it's your duty to try and learn about these things so that you're better prepared for what's about to come. Some symptoms are quite common and experienced by all pregnant women, while some can be rare and out of the blue—at the end of the day, every woman has a unique pregnancy experience. As hormones start flooding the mother's body, fatigue is one of the first symptoms they experience, along with nausea. We'll go into the details one by one starting with a little insight into ovulation and what it means.

Ovulation

In very simple terms, ovulation is when a mature egg is released from the woman's ovary. Once the egg comes out, it travels down the Fallopian tube and remains there for anywhere between 12 to 24 hours (Bellefonds, 2022). This is also where the egg can be fertilized if it meets the sperm. Once sexual intercourse is done, sperm can stay active inside the female reproductive tract for about five days if they're in conducive conditions. Thus, the chances of getting pregnant are highest when the egg and the sperm are in the Fallopian tube simultaneously. Now, if you're wondering why it's essential to understand ovulation or the time of its occurrence, well, let me explain why. When you have sexual intercourse during the time of ovulation, the woman's chance of conceiving a child is automatically increased.

How to Detect Ovulation

The average menstrual cycle of a woman spans over 28 days, and it's usually 14 days before the start of the next menstrual cycle when ovulation begins (Marnach, 2021). But this isn't something set in stone because every person has a different cycle, and the time of ovulation can vary accordingly.

Here are some things that can be done if you want to figure out when your partner ovulates:

- If the length of the menstrual cycle is usually regular, figuring out the ovulation time is easier as it's always more or less 10–16 days before your partner's next period starts (Bellefonds, 2022).

- During the time of ovulation, one of the common symptoms a woman might see is more slippery and clearer cervical mucus.

- There might be an increase in sex drive.

- After the ovulation takes place, there's a very slight change in women's body temperature—it increases.

- Some women also experience *light cramps* in the lower abdomen area.

- Getting ovulation predictor kits can also help because there's an increase in the level of hormones during this phase.

Body Symptoms

In this section, we'll have a detailed look at the bodily manifestations of ovulation in women.

- **Slippery cervical mucus:** Just before a woman ovulates, the cervical mucus changes in consistency. It becomes stretchy and wet and a lot clearer. Similarly, once the ovulation period is over, the mucus becomes cloudy and thicker, and the amount also decreases.

- **Cervical changes:** The position of the cervix is a very noticeable sign of ovulation. Before I give you any further detail, you must know what a cervix is—it's the neck-like region between the uterus and vagina that can stretch and accommodate the passage of the child during childbirth. Usually, the cervix is closed, firm, and positioned low. But during ovulation, it goes back up, becomes a little bit softer, and opens up to allow the passage of sperm into the reproductive tract.

- **Increased basal body temperature:** The basal body temperature (BBT) of a woman, undergoes fluctuations throughout the cycle owing to changes in hormone levels. But how will it help you determine whether your partner is ovulating or not? Here's how. Before ovulation, women have a high level of estrogen in their blood. Once ovulation occurs, progesterone increases, preparing the female body for reproduction, and a side effect of it's an increase in BBT. So, in short, just before ovulation, the BBT will be at its lowest, but once ovulation occurs, the BBT will start increasing.

- **Mild cramping:** If your partner is experiencing mild cramping in the weeks before the menstrual cycle starts, it's a sign that they have started ovulating and are fertile. The pain is usually felt on one side of the lower abdomen region. The side is determined by the ovary, which is releasing the egg.

- **Increased sex drive:** As women approach their ovulation phase, they experience an increase in libido. Research suggests that this increased sex drive period is when the luteinizing hormone (LH) is produced in the female body and lasts for approximately six days (Bullivant et al., 2004).

- **Tender breasts:** Tender breasts and sore nipples don't just occur during the ovulatory period but during various phases of the cycle as well. But the soreness during ovulation is linked to the rise in progesterone levels.

- **Frequent urination:** During the fertile window, some women experience frequent urination and this is linked to the sudden simultaneous spike and drop in certain hormones' levels in the body.

- **Fatigue:** When ovulation sets in, the level of progesterone rises. This directly impacts another set of hormones responsible for the sleep-wake cycle— cortisol and melatonin. The levels of both these hormones in the body decrease, making women feel tired. Fatigue can feel like a bone-crushing symptom in early pregnancy too when your partner might not feel like doing anything at all. They might feel their energy returning once they enter the second trimester.

- **Morning sickness:** Even though morning sickness isn't a common sign of ovulation, it can affect expecting moms. During ovulation, the progesterone levels aren't high enough to make the woman feel nauseous. But when they conceive successfully, that's when the queasy feeling starts setting in with the rise in hormones.

- **Food aversions:** Are you seeing your partner feeling uneasy at the smell of food every morning? Well, during ovulation, women generally have less appetite, but the smell of food doesn't bother them. When they start getting bothered by the smell, it's usually a sign that they have reached the fifth week of pregnancy. During this time, their senses are heightened, and hormones fluctuate, which leads to this uneasy feeling.

Changes in the Baby

It's quite natural for you to have questions in your mind when you're a new dad and trust me, babies grow really fast. I am a father of two, and I didn't even realize how fast the nine months flew by. So, here's some insight into the development of the baby during the first four weeks that will also give you a basic idea of what is happening inside your partner's body!

It's Growing Fast

During this time, the cells grow very rapidly as they adapt to a myriad of functions. The embryo may appear small, but it has already developed two layers—the epiblast and the hypoblast. Over the next six weeks, all the other organs of the baby will develop from these two layers. Amazing, isn't it? This is also a very crucial phase for the development of the baby, and it's susceptible to even the most minute changes. Hence, help your partner steer clear of substances that involve unsafe chemicals, drugs, smoking, and alcohol.

Since you've taken the oath to be an equal partner in this journey, you have to ensure that your partner isn't prone to overheating. It has been seen in numerous cases that high temperatures during this phase lead to neural tube defects. This is also why women are recommended not to go into hot tubs, steam baths, and saunas during their pregnancy, no matter how comfortable the idea sounds. You also need to go easy on the caffeine.

Formation of a Primitive Placenta

By the end of the fourth week, the outer cells of the embryo start to tunnel into the uterus. This enables the formation of spaces that later on allow the flow of blood and nutrients from the mother's body into the fetus. It's through the placenta that the growing baby receives its oxygen as well. Did you know that the placenta is the largest fetal organ?

Amniotic and Yolk Sacs

With your visits to the general physician, you probably have heard these two terms at least once, but you need to understand their meaning as well. As the baby grows inside the mother's womb, it needs to stay protected against all kinds of shocks; hence, the amniotic sac encloses the growing fetus. The amniotic fluid present within the sac acts as a cushion and protects the baby. On the other hand, the main function of the yolk sac is to produce the baby's first blood vessels and red blood cells.

Size Check

Right now, the best size comparison that I can provide you is that your baby is only the size of a poppy seed (but not for long)! Even though it's about 2 mm in length, the rate of growth is immense during this phase. I understand that you're probably feeling thrilled right now with the idea of becoming a new parent, but now is also the right time to start planning and adjusting to this new life. In the upcoming weeks, the embryo will soon develop a neural tube from which the spine and brain will develop. Thus, the neural tube is often referred to as the building block of fetal development.

How Can You Support Them?

There's a common misconception among couples that the first trimester will fly by easily without any problems, but the first few weeks of the pregnancy are the trickiest phase, and that is exactly when your partner needs you the most. Firstly, you've just got the news that you're going to be parents—you're still wrapping your head around the news. At the same time, your partner starts experiencing the symptoms of the first weeks—morning sickness, fatigue, mood swings, and whatnot. So, what is your duty as the dad? You're there to support them. Here's what you can do.

Physically

There are two ways in which you can help your partner—physically and emotionally. First, let's see how you can help them physically.

- **Do the heavy lifting:** When a woman is pregnant, it's advised that they don't lift anything heavy; otherwise, they will end up straining their back. But if you're to run the house, there's going to come a time when you have to do some heavy lifting, so help her out!

- **Help with the domestic chores:** Previously, it was always expected of the woman that they would keep doing the household chores even while they were pregnant. But now is the time for you to show your support toward her and split the housework. Whether it's about doing the dishes, taking the trash out, or vacuuming the sofa, help her out in whatever way you can. I mentioned in the previous section that women develop a nauseated reaction in their first trimester whenever they smell food. This makes it difficult for them to prepare food as well. So, you can help your partner by cooking food during this phase so that she can avoid the smells that trigger her.

- **Take her to an OB/GYN:** Once you receive the news that you're both pregnant, it's your duty as the dad to take your partner to an OB/GYN and ensure that she gets the medical care she needs. Remember that you're even entitled to time off from your work to attend a certain number of prenatal appointments. So, make sure you fully research these rules and are aware of the options you have.

- **Be attentive to her needs:** You need to be attentive to what your partner wants. She might have mood swings sometimes, but don't take these to heart. Always remember that it could be the hormones causing it, and this phase will pass soon—it shouldn't hamper the emotional bond you both share. Most of the time, your presence is all she needs to get through these months.

Emotionally

Now, let's look at how you can be emotionally present for your partner. Pregnancy is a happy time, and it can be maintained that way only when you're both able to sustain your emotional connection throughout. So, here are some tips you should keep in mind.

- **Prepare yourself too.** People are, most of the time, so focused on moms that they forget that dads are going through an immense emotional change too. This is particularly overwhelming for dads who will experience having a baby for the first time—they don't know anything about it and thus, spend their days reading up as much as possible. So, it's important that aside from being a support for your partner, you prepare yourself too. If you're worried about something, talk about your concerns. If you don't want to stress your partner, you can talk to a therapist or a parenting coach but don't keep your feelings bottled up—that's not going to do anyone any good.

- **Read and read some more.** I have to admit, there's no alternative to reading. When you read from the right sources, you learn about a lot of stuff and no longer anticipate the unknown. You know exactly what you're about to face, and that in itself gives a sense of relief and preparedness.

- **Talk and discuss important decisions.** Maintaining the connection with your partner throughout this journey is important. If there are important decisions to be made, don't go out of your way and make them on your own. Discuss them with your partner first and arrive at a mutual solution. This will ensure a healthy relationship during this phase.

Being a Modern Dad and Emotional Planning

Being a good dad isn't easy, and for first-time dads, it can seem even more difficult. But don't worry. By the time you reach the end of this book, you'll have a clearer idea than before as to what being a modern dad means and what planning you have to do. Suppose you open any of the social media channels. In that case, you'll instantly be bombarded with picture-perfect stories or parenthood, but always remember that social media doesn't always show you what is going on behind the photo. It's a place where all problems are non-existent, and this can take a toll on new dads and sets false expectations for them.

Just like moms, dads too go through depression and anxiety during pregnancy and even after the baby is born. But admitting vulnerability is often considered against society's accepted norms, which is why you don't hear too many stories of new dads struggling to adopt their new lifestyle. What is the result of this? Dads often suffer alone!

This is why emotional planning has become even more important, and if you want to have a smooth transition into fatherhood, you cannot take it for granted. Speak out about the challenges you're facing because there's no shame to that—it's okay not to be okay. In addition to being the perfect dad, men also have to think about their employability status. They might be eligible for paternity leave, and most of them fear that it would come back at them in the form of a missed promotion which would, in turn, mean a lesser salary. The answer to all your worries is to sort your emotions and talk about them with an expert. It's okay to feel unsure and overwhelmed, but when you ask for help, an expert can help you navigate these feelings better.

Changing Roles

With the hormones constantly fluctuating, pregnant women often feel like they have gone back to their adolescent years, which is no easy task. They have to deal with physical pain, and mood swings can turn a perfectly happy day upside down. Pregnancy is a phase no woman can ever be fully prepared for, but you, as their partner, can make life a bit easier for them to adapt to their changing role.

- Pregnancy is a long journey. Growing a baby—a human being—inside the belly for nine whole months isn't a joke. For you, every day might not bring a new challenge—you might not be going through a new body transformation every day. But your partner is. So, the least you could do is show them some compassion. **Most women want their partners to be present with**

them during labor and delivery—they want emotional support. Just because she has the endurance and capability to give birth doesn't mean she'll play the role of the parent alone; hence, you must be by her side during this important day in her life.

- It's true that you probably cannot make the journey easier for your partner physically. But **it helps women if their partners are educated during the antenatal period.** This is because men rarely understand what is happening inside the female body and start making assumptions of their own. But when you acquire knowledge, you know exactly what is happening, and you'll also have the right cure for it. This will help you support your partner throughout all the physically challenging experiences.

- During pregnancy, most women experience a loss in libido. And this can make them feel that something is wrong with them. What is required here is that they need to open up about what they feel so that they can maintain a strong emotional connection with you. **A reduction in your partner's sex drive means you have to care for her all the more.** You have to ensure that she doesn't suffer from a negative self-image. At that same time, talk to your partner and engage in other kinds of intimacy because that might help them feel better about themselves.

Pregnancy can be emotionally hard for both parents, and as we proceed further into this book, I'll tell you about what each month entails and how you should deal with each one of them. The next chapter talks about the second month of pregnancy and how you fit into all of it.

Chapter 2:

Month 2—Be Her Support

System

The strongest, toughest men all have compassion. They're not heartless and cold. You have to be man enough to have compassion—to care about people and about your children. –Denzel Washington

During the nine months of pregnancy, you're your partner's biggest support system. In order to truly be there for her, you need to have some amount of compassion that will help you understand the experiences she's going through. However, the role of compassion doesn't end there. If you want to inculcate emotional intelligence in your child, you must show them your compassionate side. It has been proven time and again that children, irrespective of their gender, when they have a compassionate role model to look up to, are more *emotionally literate* and don't give in to things like peer pressure later on in their life (Hattori, 2014). Compassion will also help you break free of gender stereotypes which, in the long run, will help in the better upbringing of the child free from any judgment whatsoever.

In this chapter, we'll have a detailed look into the changes that happen in the mother and the baby in the second month of pregnancy. We'll also learn about other aspects that need to be kept in mind during this time.

Changes in the Mom

Now that your partner has reached her fifth week of the pregnancy journey, the baby is growing at quite a steady pace in her uterus. This means that she's becoming aware of some of the common discomforts of pregnancy. That being said, this is also the time when some couples choose to announce their pregnancy. Even though it's not set in stone as to when you can announce, it's entirely up to you. But the fifth week is common among couples when they choose to announce the good news to the broader community of friends and family. So, without any further ado, let's look at some of the common changes your partner will go through during this phase that you should be aware of.

- **Frequent urination.** The need to pee more often than usual is a very common thing during pregnancy. Even nocturia (frequent urination at night) is a common phenomenon in pregnancy. Now you may be wondering why your partner needs to pee more often. Well, there are a number of reasons associated with it. Firstly, when a woman is pregnant, the amount of blood present in their body becomes almost double what they usually have. The direct result of this is that the kidneys have to process more fluids. Secondly, during pregnancy, a woman's kidneys become more efficient in getting rid of all the unnecessary waste from the body, which automatically leads to frequent urination. Thirdly, you're already aware of the several hormonal changes your partner has to go through during this time. One of the effects of these changes is that the ligaments of the urethra loosen up, so they cannot hold urine for as long as they used to before. Thus, you must ensure your partner is staying hydrated at all times.

- **Tender, swollen breasts.** Another very common symptom of pregnancy in the earlier weeks is breast tenderness. They may feel tingly, sore, and swollen. Even the nipples might feel uncomfortable and extra sensitive. This is all because of progesterone and estrogen, whose levels increase during the early phase of pregnancy and prepare your partner's body for breastfeeding. The best way to provide relief to your partner is to get them the most comfortable underwear that doesn't irritate their breasts.

- **Fatigue.** This time of the pregnancy is also when the extreme levels of fatigue start setting in, and no one can tell you for sure why. However, it's most likely that hormones have a role to play here as well. As the pregnancy progresses towards the second trimester, your partner might feel their energy coming back but until then, make it easier for them to get sufficient rest. Take good care of them and lighten their load.

- **Morning sickness.** Morning sickness is often characterized by vomiting and nausea, and this particular symptom affects different women at different times during their pregnancy. When the levels of human chorionic gonadotropin (hCG) start to show in your partner's blood from week five, that's when the morning sickness appears, and it peaks sometime around the ninth week because that's when the hormone is at its highest levels. Did you know that 70% of women will face morning sickness during their pregnancy? (Gates, 2021). So, it's quite a common phenomenon indeed. If your partner is suffering too much, make sure you talk with her healthcare provider to find a solution.

- **Food aversions.** Even though food aversions can be quite an unpleasant experience for the woman, they're very common during pregnancy. Even though they go away during the later months, there's a possibility that your partner's appetite can be out of tune. Some common food aversions include anything with a strong smell, spicy foods, dairy products, meat, eggs, coffee, and so on. Even though there isn't sufficient research to back the claims, most experts believe that a rise in hCG has something to do with these food aversions.

- **Bleeding or spotting.** Very light amounts of vaginal bleeding, also known as spotting, are sometimes seen in women during the early weeks of pregnancy. However, you must remember that continued bleeding must be taken seriously. Some non-serious reasons that can lead to spotting are implantation of the egg into the uterus, but this mostly happens in the first 6–12 days and not in the fifth or sixth week of pregnancy. During this time, the most likely reasons for spotting can be hormones, infection, or sex.

- **Metallic taste.** When there's a rise in estrogen in the blood, women experience a metallic taste in their mouths. You can help your partner combat this feeling by asking them to eat acidic and tart food items, or simply gargling with a mild solution of water and baking soda or salt. Chewing sugarless mint gum also helps. There's a myth that the baby's gender can be predicted through this metallic taste, but there's no scientific evidence to back this up.

- **Strange dreams.** Next, let's talk about your partner having strange dreams during the second month of her pregnancy. There's nothing to worry about because this is very common and usually happens out of anxiety. As a woman becomes pregnant, she goes through a lot of physical and mental changes. Common pregnancy dreams often have babies, water, and baby animals in them. However, they can have bad and erotic dreams too. If your partner is having too many bad dreams, there might be some psychological aspect to it, and they might be worried about something. It's better to talk to their healthcare provider about this.

- **Headaches.** It's common for women to experience headaches during the second month, or rather, the first trimester of pregnancy. Changing sleeping habits and light exercises can often help. These headaches occur because some women are more sensitive to the rise in estrogen in their bodies; for others, it happens because of increased blood volume. Another common reason is that during pregnancy, women start cutting back on caffeine, and this sudden lifestyle change can also trigger headaches. Some other possible causes include allergies, migraine, hunger, depression, stress, eye strain, sinus congestion, general fatigue, and dehydration.

So, now that you're more aware of the changes in the mother's body, let's move on to baby development during the second month of pregnancy.

Changes in the Baby

Now that your partner has reached the second month of pregnancy, the baby will develop many features that we'll discuss in this section. By the end of the second month, you might notice that your partner's clothes fit more snugly than usual. This is normal because the uterus is gradually making space for the baby's development. So, let's take a brief look at the changes happening in the growing fetus.

Nerves, Bones, and Muscles Developing in Your Baby's Fingers and Toes

This is a crucial time for your baby's development since the nerves start developing and spreading through the fetus' body. The nerves form connections between tissues and muscles and also between each other. They also connect other parts of the body like ears and eyes.

The neural crest of the fetus is located just around the edges of the neural tube. This crest, along with the spinal cord and the brain, leads to the development of millions of nerves in the fetus, which later on branches out all over the body.

Your Baby Is Moving Now, You Won't Feel It Move

Congratulations! At about eight weeks, your baby starts moving, but this isn't the time when the mother can feel the baby moving. These are some initial movements that are often described as spontaneous stretches and twitches. These movements are visible when you take your partner to perform an ultrasound scan around the seventh or eighth week of pregnancy. The mother will be able to feel the fetus moving when they reach about 16 weeks into pregnancy. However, until then, the movements are very nuanced and thus, not strong enough for your partner to notice.

The Baby Is Getting Ready to Breathe

Next up, another very prominent change that happens in the fetus during the eighth week of pregnancy is that they start developing the respiratory system. The lungs start developing, and breathing tubes come out of the baby's throat and then branch out into the developing lungs. However, you must know that during the pregnancy, the babies get their supply of oxygen through the placenta. Hence, they only need their lungs once they're born and not before that.

At about six weeks into pregnancy, a small pouch-like structure called the *lung bud* develops, which is the first sign of the development of the respiratory system in the fetus. This develops in the front wall of the tube which later forms the baby's esophagus. In about another week's time, the bud separates into two, where one bud represents each lung. Gradually, the windpipe starts to develop between the lung buds.

Towards the end of the sixth week, the bronchi or tube system is created when the two lung buds start branching internally. In the beginning, only two bronchi form, and they connect to each of the lungs. As time passes, small branches come off the main bronchi, and more such bronchi are added with time.

Size Check

By the end of the second month, your baby is about the size of a kidney bean, roughly 0.62 in, and weighs 0.71 oz (Gates, 2022). They grow really fast. By now, they have muscles, bones, toes, fingers, legs, and arms. In short, you can say, even though they're small, they look quite similar to a baby you would bring home from the hospital. Their organs and inner workings continue to develop at this stage, as do their facial features. At the same time, the fetus' nose and the upper jaw have started taking proper shape during this phase. You can also say that the tadpole-like appearance of the fetus you had seen in the previous chapter gradually fades in the second month.

What to Expect at Your Prenatal Test This Month

Some couples go for their first prenatal visit as early as the sixth week, but the eighth week is the most common time. That being said, you must remember that this is probably going to be the longest and also most comprehensive doctor's appointment you'll ever take with your partner. Are you feeling anxious about what to expect when you visit the doctor? Well, don't worry, you're not alone! I still remember the first prenatal visit with my wife and boy, I was so worried about what the doctor was going to say. But it went pretty well. So, based on my experience, here are some things that you should be expecting on your first prenatal test this month:

- **There will be a check-up.** This mainly consists of a general health exam where your partner's lungs, heart, abdomen, and breasts will be checked. After that, the doctor will check her blood pressure (this is a must!). This blood pressure record will serve as a baseline for all other future appointments. Your partner's weight and height will be recorded. Then, the doctor will look for any swelling or presence of varicose veins and note it down as a baseline for future appointments. A thorough pelvic exam will be done which will help determine the size of the uterus and also the size and shape of the pelvis.

- **Confirmation of the pregnancy.** Once all the general check-ups are out of the way, the confirmation of your pregnancy then comes. Since you've come all the way to the doctor's office, it's only natural that you've already gotten a positive result in the home kit, but even then, your healthcare provider will do blood and urine tests to check for the levels of hCG.

- **There will be a battery of other tests.** Every pregnant woman has to go through a routine of several other tests. Some of these tests are absolutely necessary, while others are prescribed under certain specific conditions. The most common tests include:

  o *Urine test.* Your partner's urine sample will be taken to check for her levels of bacteria, blood, white blood cells, glucose, and protein.

  o *Bloodwork.* One blood sample will be taken to determine your partner's Rh status and blood type and check if she has anemia. The blood levels will then also be checked for the presence of antibodies. This helps determine her immunity levels to diseases like chicken pox and rubella, and whether there's a vitamin D deficiency.

  o *STD tests.* Another important set of tests is the sexually transmitted disease (STD) tests which are done to see if your partner is carrying any STDs like syphilis, hepatitis B, HIV, chlamydia, and gonorrhea.

  o *Genetic carrier screening.* Some people perform this screening before conception, but if you haven't, then your partner will be tested to see if there are any common genetic conditions that she's a carrier of, for example, Tay-Sachs disease, thalassemia, sickle cell anemia, cystic fibrosis, and so on.

o **Pap smear.** This test is done to check for any abnormal cells in the cervix of pregnant women.

o **Blood sugar test.** If a person is a high-risk patient for gestational diabetes, the doctor might suggest getting this test. This can happen if your partner has a family history of gestational diabetes or if she had a previous pregnancy where she had it, etc.

- **You'll be provided with an official countdown:** This is probably the most exciting part of the first prenatal check-up! But for this, you have to mention your partner's last period date and the day you conceived. This will help the doctor in calculating your due date. They will also check the uterus and cervix for the approximate gestational age of the pregnancy, and an ultrasound will make things easier.

- **You'll have a chat about your partner's health and the baby:** Your primary healthcare provider's only aim is to provide you with the best care possible. They will want to know all about you and your partner's medical history. Once you've given them all this information, it's time you get all your doubts cleared. They will also try their best to fill you in on the gaps and get you up to speed on how to best care for the mother and the growing fetus. It always helps if you take notes because sometimes there's so much information that new dads tend to forget.

Now that you have a pretty good idea of what is going to happen on your first prenatal visit, you might even get a glimpse of your baby because most practitioners do an ultrasound (because that's the most accurate way of dating the pregnancy).

How Can You Help?

Being a first-time dad, I've compiled some of the things that you can do during this second month that will make life a little bit easier for your partner:

- I mentioned before in this chapter that spotting is common in the second month, but if there's bleeding and your partner is tense about it, your first duty is to calm them down. After that, take them to the primary healthcare provider or the OB/GYN under whom she's seeking treatment.

- It's important that you ensure your partner stays nourished all throughout the day. Morning sickness makes it difficult to keep the food in as it is. So the best thing that you can do is help them eat small meals throughout the day. Get them their favorite meals that are rich in nutrients.

- Take your partner for an ultrasound. The second month is when you should go for your first prenatal check-up, and all the details related to it have already been discussed in the previous section.

- There are several foods that women need to skip during pregnancy. Research what those foods are. Take some time to find out what's safe to eat and what's not.

- If your partner has a day job, take some time out to visit them at their workplace to ensure it's safe for them to work there. Some jobs can indeed be hazardous for pregnant women. If her job involves her being in constant exposure to harmful chemicals or radiation, make her understand that it's not good for the baby and then politely ask her to talk to her boss about it. Every woman is eligible for maternity leave.

- Help your partner to reduce their stress levels as much as possible. Stress can have some really bad effects on the growing baby. Help them take breaks from time to time by helping around the house or holding weekly house parties and surrounding themselves with positive people.

- If you're unsure which tests must be done, always consult a healthcare provider first.

- Pay attention to whether your partner is sleeping well. Pregnancy is a time when women feel extremely exhausted. However, at the same time, they also face a host of sleep problems like insomnia, snoring, leg cramps, heartburn, nausea, and frequent urination. You can help them by developing a sleep routine, choosing the right pillows, and adjusting the diet to include food items that promote better sleep.

- Ask your partner to use pregnancy-safe sunscreen. Using sunscreen during pregnancy is an absolute must, but most women ignore it and then suffer from a condition known as melasma. If you don't want the same happening to your partner, help them choose a broad-spectrum sunscreen that is safe for pregnant women.

- Some women can become very demotivated and acquire an inferior sense of self-image owing to pregnancy weight gain. So, you need to have that talk with your partner. Gaining weight during pregnancy is completely normal, and you need to give them emotional support during this time so that they don't feel bad about their changing body.

Starting around the second month, your partner will start noticing several other changes in her body. For example, her breasts will start becoming bigger and keep growing throughout the pregnancy to accommodate breastfeeding. The breasts might also develop stretch marks and might feel itchy. You can consult her health provider for ointments that can relieve the itchiness.

Sex During Pregnancy

Unless and until your partner's doctor or midwife has advised you not to have sex, it's perfectly safe to have it during this time of the pregnancy. Most fathers and even mothers are concerned about whether it will hurt the baby but trust me, it won't. The amniotic fluid present in the uterus protects the developing fetus. As long as your partner doesn't have any placenta problems or preterm labor, sexual activity doesn't affect the baby in any way. However, there's something else that you should keep in mind—your partner's sexual desire and level of comfort often changes during the pregnancy.

There might be times when you both feel like having sex and thoroughly enjoy it, and there will also be times when your partner doesn't seem interested at all. In that case, you have to find other ways of making love. Remember that sex isn't the only form of showing affection or love to your partner. The most important thing during pregnancy is to solidify your bond with your wife and talk about your feelings. Rest assured, if the pregnancy is proceeding as it should, there's no chance of your baby going into early labor or your partner encountering a miscarriage just because you had sex.

However, there are certain times when sex needs to be avoided in pregnancy, and they're as follows:

- if your partner's water has broken, where having sex can increase the risk of infection.

- if your partner previously had early labors or if you're having twins and she is in the later stage of pregnancy

- if your partner has some cervical problems

That being said, even when sex is safe, it might not be as easy as it used to be before. So, it's time you experiment with some positions with your partner to find what is working out for both of you.

Her Feelings

Women undergo a wide range of emotions due to the hormonal buildup that they experience during pregnancy. They can be extremely moody at times as well. And being a first-time dad, all of this can be overwhelming to deal with at times. So, here are some things you can do to help her deal with her feelings and make her feel comfortable:

- **When she's blissfully happy.** Not all emotions are bad; some are good. There will be times when she experiences a surge of estrogen, which automatically makes her feel happy and gives her a sense of well-being. And then there are those women who had been trying to have a baby for a really long time, and now that they finally have one in their belly, they can't seem to contain their excitement. During these times, you need to be with them and enjoy with them because, during these moments, you both are going to make some really happy memories that will last forever!

- **When she's irritable and teary.** Anxiety, sadness, and irritability are some of the very prominent symptoms that women experience when hormones fluctuate in the second month. What will be your role as a husband? You need to explain to your partner that whatever they're going through is normal, and these are heavy emotions to deal with. Make sure your partner follows a healthy diet (women often tend to overlook the nutrition aspect when they're moody), and you can ask them to do some light exercise. Good emotional well-being comes out of good physical well-being. However, if your partner has a history of depression and if you feel she's going back into that spiral, you need to take her to a specialist instead of trying to deal with it yourself.

- **When she feels sexual.** If your partner feels sexual all of a sudden and if her doctor has said that having sex won't affect the baby, then go for it!

- **When she feels extremely tired.** Pregnancy is a time when the crushing exhaustion sets in out of nowhere, and you might find your partner complaining about the fatigue all day long. You can teach her to compartmentalize her day so that she can get her chores done or any pending office work and fantasize about baby names or read a book if she wants to. And if her body simply doesn't want to, allow her to rest and help her around the house as much as you can. However, if she's extremely sluggish, you might want to bring that up with the doctor. They will suggest a test for anemia to rule that out.

You must learn to recognize when the emotions are normal and when it's a mental health problem. More than one in eight women undergoes anxiety or depression during their pregnancy, and seeking medical help is the right way to go about it (National Childbirth Trust, 2019).

Your Feelings

With the newest member of your family coming in a few more months, there's a surge of emotions all around. Amidst all this, it's equally important to pay attention to what is happening inside your mind. Pregnancy and love aren't a very good combination at all times, and even though some moments can be inexplicably close, there will be others where you might feel disconnected. In this section, we're going to talk about some issues dads face during pregnancy and what they can do to address those issues:

- **Your partner is getting too clingy.** During the time of pregnancy, a woman's emotions are affected in a profound manner owing to the constant hormone fluctuation. During early pregnancy, several women feel a sense of abandonment which is why even the most independent women will start becoming too clingy, and this can take a toll on your mental health as a first-time dad. Your partner might be making unreasonable demands all the time and wanting all your attention. It would be best if you let her know from time to time that you need your personal space too. It's not that you're not there for her, but at times you need your own space to be able to breathe.

- **Both of you might not be on the same page about everything.** Do you feel that you have too many fights all of a sudden? Well, it's quite common in pregnant couples. It's best if you don't take everything to heart and overthink these situations. Your partner still loves you—it's just that even they're overwhelmed by this new phase of life.

- **You're feeling left out.** The whole pregnancy journey is mostly about women, and it's very common for dads to feel left out even when they have equal rights to be part of this memorable time. Aside from a few congratulations, dads don't receive much, and that's the sad part. Hence, you both should work together to set aside some me-time to keep your bond strong. This will be your non-baby time.

- **Sex might slow down.** Some people might argue that sex has nothing to do with emotional intimacy but let me tell you, it does. As the months pass by and the baby bump keeps getting bigger, your partner may not be interested in sex as she was before. But keeping your physical connection strong during pregnancy is essential to maintaining a strong emotional bond. This may or may not be in the form of sex. You can work it out between yourselves to choose something you're both comfortable with.

At the end of the day, you have to remember that she's still the same woman you fell in love with no matter how different she feels now. This is just a phase of nine months, and after that, things will slowly start going back to the usual (of course, with a new family member by your side!).

Mindfulness and Being Her Support System

Since pregnancy is such a stressful time, being a good partner means being her support system, and in this section, I'll guide you on how you can be that. Going to antenatal classes and reading pregnancy books is definitely a good place to start, but there's so much more that we'll discuss here.

Positive Self-Talk

Women often experience anxiety during pregnancy, and positive self-talk can keep them from feeling overwhelmed. It's very easy to fall into a downward spiral of mental breakdown and negativity, but it's your duty as the partner to support them with positive vibes so that they don't constantly replay past events or harp on imperfections. Being stressed releases more amounts of cortisol which can harm the pregnancy.

Help your partner always see the bigger picture instead of focusing on small day-to-day negative things. There might be some setbacks in the pregnancy which are only situational and temporary, but there's no need to get fixated on them. Help them positively reframe their negative thoughts. Step out of the cycle of perfectionism. Everything need not be so perfect. It's okay if some things are imperfect. For example, you don't need to have everything done in the baby's room before it comes. If you've done only some things, it's completely okay. You can do the rest with time. You have to make your partner see the world in a positive light so that they can stop beating themselves up over petty matters.

Affirmations

The importance of affirmations during pregnancy cannot be stressed enough. These are short, positive sentences, and they're always said in the present tense. You can encourage your partner to repeat some positive affirmations with you throughout the day. Some examples of these affirmations are as follows:

- My body is perfectly capable of giving birth to our baby.

- I am okay with the changes in my body.

- I am beautiful just the way I am.

- I am healthy, and so is my baby.

- I can endure everything that comes my way.

- I am looking forward to the birthing experience.

When you remind your partner of all the positive things about pregnancy, it will free them of anxiety and worry. On the other hand, when these negative emotions go unchecked, that is when they cause irreparable harm to pregnant women leading to stress and depression.

You've Got This

Don't worry. I know you're wondering whether what you're doing is enough or not, but trust me, you've got this! Sometimes, all your partner needs you to do is *show up!* Know when she has her doctor appointments and simply be there for her—that in itself is a lot of mental and emotional support.

Actively participate in all the pregnancy-related decisions that you both have to make. Go to the antenatal and birthing classes with her. And most importantly, always engage in open communication.

Your partner should always feel like they can share anything they want with you. This means even if they're feeling emotional, sad, or depressed—they should be able to communicate that to you effortlessly. Remember that pregnancy isn't always happy because, for some women, it can also bring up feelings of fear and self-doubt. Hence, you always need to be there for her.

Antenatal Care Chart

Antenatal care refers to the regular supervision that a pregnant woman has to go through. You've already learned about your first prenatal test in the earlier part of this chapter. In this section, I'll provide a chart that will give you a rough idea of what's to follow.

16–24 weeks	Your partner will be asked about any discomfort she's facing. A general and systemic physical examination will be done. The height of the fundus of the uterus will be noted to compare with the gestational age. Blood and urine tests will be done to test for sugar and protein levels. An ultrasound will also be performed to exclude fetal anomalies.

24–32 weeks	Your partner will be asked about any discomfort she's facing. General and systemic physical examinations will be done. The height of the fundus of the uterus will be noted to compare with the gestational age. Symphysis-fundal height & abdominal girth is also noted down. The fetal heart is auscultated. Blood and urine tests will be done to test for sugar and protein levels. A blood GCT test is also done.
32–36 weeks	Your partner will be asked about any discomfort she's facing. A general and systemic physical examination will be done. The height of the fundus of the uterus will be noted to compare with the gestational age. Symphysis-fundal height & abdominal girth is also noted down. The fetal heart is auscultated. Lie, position, and presentation of the fetus will be recorded at this stage. Blood and urine tests will be done to test for sugar and protein levels.
36–40 weeks	Your partner will be asked about any discomfort she's

	facing. A general and systemic physical examination will be done. The height of the fundus of the uterus will be noted to compare with the gestational age. Symphysis-fundal height & abdominal girth is also noted down. The fetal heart is auscultated. Lie, position, and presentation of the fetus will be recorded at this stage. Amniotic fluid volume is clinically assessed. A pelvic assessment is done, and the cervical condition is checked. Blood and urine tests will be done to test for sugar and protein levels. A biophysical profile will be created after doing an ultrasound.
After 40 weeks	Your partner will be asked about any discomfort she's facing. A general and systemic physical examination will be done. The height of the fundus of the uterus will be noted to compare with the gestational age. Symphysis-fundal height & abdominal girth is also noted down. The fetal heart is auscultated. Lie, position, and presentation of the fetus will be recorded at this stage. Amniotic fluid

	volume is clinically assessed. Pelvic assessment is done to rule out cephalopelvic disproportion or CPD, and the cervical condition is checked. Blood and urine tests will be done to test for sugar and protein levels. A biophysical profile will be created after doing an ultrasound at least two times a week.

By now, you probably have a clear idea about what goes on in the second month of pregnancy. The next chapter talks about pregnancy at three months and your ever-evolving role.

Chapter 3:

Month 3—One Trimester Done Already!

The greatest mark of a father is how he treats his children when no one is looking. –Dan Pearce

Fathers play a unique role throughout the pregnancy. Loving fathers not only love the growing baby dearly but always put the needs of the mother at the top of their priority list. They offer their love without any reservation whatsoever. Loving fathers love the growing baby unconditionally, and they know that the child needs someone it can look up to. They still respect the child's mother even if they're divorced. They do their best to provide for the family. Yes, sometimes it can be tough, especially when fathers lose their jobs, but they try their best to offer a stable home through their affection and love. In this chapter, I'll walk you through the different aspects of the third month of pregnancy (yes, you've already reached the first trimester!). So, buckle up because there's a lot to learn!

Changes in the Mom

Congratulations! You're almost done with the first trimester. Your partner may still not physically appear pregnant to people, but several changes are going on in her body. Let's take a look at some of those.

- **Warning signs.** Before we go into the changes that a pregnant woman experiences during this phase, let's talk about some of the warning signs you should be aware of.

  o Lower back pain is one of the first warning signs during this phase—there's not too much to worry about because it's usually linked with hormones and stress. However, if back pain is accompanied by other symptoms like vaginal bleeding, burning sensation during urination, and fever, then you must contact the doctor right away.

  o The next warning sign that you should be aware of is vaginal bleeding. Some amount of spotting is normal, but if your partner is experiencing heavy bleeding, then it might be a sign of ectopic pregnancy or even a miscarriage. However, in case of a miscarriage, the woman will also experience very bad cramps.

  o If your partner is facing persistent itching in the vaginal region, she should not feel shy to bring up the problem. You should call up her primary care doctor and let them know because it can be a sign of STDs or some treatable infections.

- **Exhaustion.** When your partner is about nine weeks pregnant, exhaustion can completely take over her body. When she stops moving, she'll feel like nodding off every now and then, and she'll literally have to fight that urge if she wants to stay awake for the day. It's advisable that you ask her to sleep whenever she can.

- **Food cravings.** Pregnancy is a time when the woman undergoes an extreme amount of hormonal changes, and this leads to food cravings. However, some experts have linked these cravings to the fact that moms-to-be have an increased need for nutrition when they're pregnant. There are other experts who think cravings during pregnancy don't have such a simple explanation. It's okay for your partner to indulge in their favorite food items when the cravings start setting in but they should try everything in moderation. There's also an unusual condition some pregnant women face known as pica, whereby they start craving non-food substances such as clay, dirt, or even laundry starch. If you notice your partner going through such a state, you must let her healthcare provider know.

- **Constipation.** It's said that up to 50% of pregnant women will experience constipation when pregnant (Millard, 2021). It's usually the result of an expanding uterus and decreased activity levels, coupled with the influx of hormones in the body. Talk with your partner's healthcare provider about the type of foods you can include in her diet that will ease bowel movements. Typically, high-fiber foods are advisable. She might also be asked to switch her prenatal vitamins especially if she had been taking a lot of iron supplements lately.

- **Nasal congestion.** Nasal congestion around the ninth week of pregnancy, also known as pregnancy rhinitis, happens because the mucus membranes inside the nose undergo inflammation. This usually makes it uncomfortable for your partner to fall asleep and can last for a few weeks. Over-the-counter decongestant sprays often help but make sure you talk with the healthcare provider first.

These were some of the symptoms that are new for your partner in the third month of pregnancy but now, let's talk about some other symptoms that your partner should be aware of in the 9th and 10th week of pregnancy.

- **Morning sickness peaks at around weeks 9 and 10.** The third month will be the peak time for morning sickness, and your partner will most definitely be going through a hard time. Some experts are of the belief that morning sickness is a way for the female body to protect the fetus from toxins, and this belief is reinforced by the fact that the first trimester is also when the baby's most vital organs are in their early phases of development. Nausea may not only strike in the morning but any time of the day.

- **Abdominal aches because of expanding size.** Since your partner's womb is expanding, it's common to experience mild abdominal aches during this stage. As the bump keeps growing, the ligaments keep stretching, and women often complain that it feels like they're experiencing mild menstrual pain.

- **Visible veins.** You may be noticing some new veins on your partner across their belly, breast, and chest area. These new veins appear as the body produces more blood to support the fetus; the veins become more visible and enlarged in size. As the uterus grows in size, some women also develop varicose veins in their legs.

- **Dizziness.** A woman's body is working way harder than usual when she's pregnant because the body is trying to pump more and more blood. The cardiovascular and nervous systems of the body are able to adjust to these rapid changes; however, it might happen that from time to time, enough blood may not flow into the brain. This is what makes your partner feel lightheaded or dizzy. When this happens, you must ask her to sit down or, better yet, lie down until she feels better.

- **May start to show.** Your partner's midsection will thicken, and she may start to show that she's pregnant. She will also experience slight bloating and weight gain during this phase. This is the right time to shift to maternity clothes. She needs skirts and pants that have stretchy waistbands and room for growth.

- **Heartburn.** Even women who have never had prior experience of heartburn complain of the problem during pregnancy. And let me tell you, it's not at all a good feeling. Heartburn feels something like a burning sensation somewhere between the bottom of the breast bone and the lower throat. You should ensure that your partner avoids food items like processed meats, mint products, vinegar, mustard, tomatoes, citrus fruits and juices, chocolate, caffeine, and carbonated drinks if they experience heartburn.

- **Conflicting emotions.** The emotions take on a rollercoaster ride during the third month. In general, mood swings hit the worst between the 6th and 10th weeks of pregnancy. Your partner may feel anxious, slightly nervous, or even confused. Make sure you spend enough time with them and talk about what they're feeling.

- **Pregnancy weight gain.** Your partner may gain some weight during this time, but there's no need to worry because this is completely natural. In general, 3–4 lb of weight gain is common among women during the first trimester (Johnson, 2020).

- **Increased sex drive.** With the hormones skyrocketing at this time of pregnancy, it's quite natural for your partner to have an increased sex drive.

Staying aware of your partner's symptoms will help you remain involved in the pregnancy and also help you understand what your partner is going through.

Changes in the Baby

Now, the 12-week mark is said to be the turning point for baby development. All the body systems and key vital organs have started forming. Let's take a detailed look at all that is happening inside the womb.

- **Small movements start.** Around the 12th week, the fetus starts to make small movements by curling its toes, closing its hands, and forming a fist.

- **Tiny fingernails growing.** By the 12th week, your baby has already developed its unique fingerprint, and not only that but their fingers and toes have also started developing small fingernails.

- **Intestines.** Around the seventh week of pregnancy, the esophagus and stomach start forming. The intestines of your baby develop quite fast, and they protrude into the umbilical cord. Very soon, the walls of the abdominal cavity will close, and the intestines will find their way into the abdomen of the baby. By the 10th week, the rectum and the anus have fully formed, and the kidneys are also able to make urine. What's even better is that the pancreas is also able to produce insulin at this stage.

- **Size check.** During the third month, your baby is about the size of a lime with an approximate length of about 2.13 in. and a weight of about 2.05 oz (Miles, 2021a).

How Can You Help?

The third month is one of the best times for making pregnancy announcements, but at the same time, you must keep in mind that your partner is going through a range of emotions. In this section, we'll explore the various ways in which you can help them during this phase.

Make Sure They're Not Being Discriminated Against for Their Pregnancy at Their Workplace

Based on the information available from the U.S. Department of Labor, if you consider the total workforce in the country, 50% are women (Robinson, 2020). It has also been found that 85% of working women are going to become mothers at some point in their careers. Studies have also shown that more work needs to be done in the case of pregnant women who are recruited as frontline workers, are female firefighters, or are temporarily disabled but are pregnant. They should be given disability leave or alternate assignments suited for them.

If a woman is pregnant and, owing to this pregnancy, they're unable to perform their job the way they usually do, the employer must not treat them any differently. But the situation on the ground isn't so. In the past decade alone, the Fair Employment Practices Agencies and Equal Employment Opportunity Commission stated that approximately 50,000 pregnancy discrimination claims were filed (Robinson, 2020).

Shocking, isn't it? So, you must ensure that your partner isn't undergoing the same thing at her workplace.

Make Sure They Don't Stay Standing for Long Periods

Women are usually capable of doing all the everyday physical activities. In fact, with the doctor's approval, your partner can even engage in some light to moderate exercises; however, there are some physical demands that can put the growing baby at risk. One such physical demand is standing for a long period of time. It can lead to preterm labor but during the third month of pregnancy, what is more common is that prolonged standing increases the chances of a miscarriage. Hence, you should always make sure that your partner is well-rested and isn't standing for long periods unnecessarily.

Help Them Stay Positive

Women usually tend to worry when they're pregnant. But excessive worrying isn't good for their health. It can take a mental, physical, and emotional toll on them. On the other hand, when a woman maintains a positive attitude, they sleep enough, eats well, and stays active—all of which are essential for a healthy pregnancy. When she's positive, she's also able to enjoy and focus on how miraculously her body is changing to accommodate this new family member, and it also helps her develop a positive relationship with the unborn baby.

At the same time, I want to make it clear to you that developing a positive attitude doesn't mean that your partner has to bury her head in the sand. Stress is understandable during pregnancy because of the whirlwind of changes that the woman undergoes. It would be unrealistic to expect a woman to completely ignore these changes or not think about them. But what you can do is encourage them to discuss things with you or if they have any concerns, ask them to bring them up so that you both can talk it out, and it will make her feel much lighter.

Be Attentive Towards Their Nutrition

Getting enough nutrition is extremely important during pregnancy. You, as her partner, must ensure that she's taking all her meals and prenatal vitamins as directed by the doctor. Their diet should be rich in:

- **Calcium.** The importance of calcium during pregnancy cannot be stressed enough. The baby needs calcium for the development of muscles, nerves, teeth, and obviously strong bones! Moreover, when the mother has adequate levels of calcium in her body, it automatically reduces the risk of encountering several complications in pregnancy. As a recommended limit, women who are aged 19 years and above require 1,000 mg of calcium per day (Gates, 2022).

- **Magnesium.** Magnesium is one such nutrient that is needed for the development of almost every system in the body. On average, a woman needs 350–400 mg of magnesium daily when she's pregnant (Dasher, 2021). To be specific, magnesium plays an irreplaceable role in muscle and nerve function and also helps maintain proper levels of blood pressure in the body.

- **Vitamin D.** This particular vitamin plays a crucial role in bone health, healthy cell division, and the functioning of the immune system. It's also important for the metabolism and absorption of calcium and phosphorus. If a pregnant woman is deficient in Vitamin D, it increases their chances of preeclampsia.

Help Them With Their Skin Care

You've probably heard of the "pregnancy glow" by now, and yes, it's real but women often don't see it until the later stages of pregnancy; hence, they have to take care of their skin to protect it from issues. With the hormonal influx and body changes, several skin changes might happen like stretch marks, itchy skin, rashes, melasma, varicose veins, and acne. Dealing with all these issues on her own can seem overwhelming for your partner. So, you should always be by her side, helping her with her skincare routine in whatever capacity you can.

Remind Them to Drink Water 10 to 12 Times a Day

Water has a host of benefits during pregnancy, and it's recommended that your partner drinks 10 to 12 cups every day. It not only maintains the digestive system but also ensures the proper formation of the amniotic fluid that protects the fetus from harm. Water is also important to flush out the toxins and wastes from your partner's body. It helps in carrying nutrients, building new tissue, and producing extra blood. It will also keep your partner energized. Another important role performed by water is that it keeps urinary tract infections at bay.

Take Care of Yourself in Case of Sympathetic Pregnancy Symptoms

Are you not feeling well or feeling queasy alongside your partner? Well, there's a term for it, and it's completely natural. It's known as sympathetic pregnancy symptom or couvade syndrome. Some people often confuse it with the fact that the male partner is copycatting the pregnant woman to gain attention. But it's not that. Couvade syndrome happens when the male partner in the relationship is understanding of the problems of the pregnant partner to the extent that they physically feel their discomfort out of empathy. If you're going through something similar, don't hesitate to ask for help. Be patient with yourself, and don't be harsh towards yourself for feeling sick or low. Pregnancy can be surprising and even takes a mental and physical toll on the father-to-be.

The Changing Dynamics of Your Home and Preparing for a New Member

Your family is currently undergoing a transition—and bringing a baby into the fold isn't always easy. In this section, I'll guide you through the family dynamics that work in the background and how you can navigate it smoothly.

- **Adjusting expectations.** When a baby is on the way, you and your partner will have to make some adjustments, and you also need to make some tweaks to your expectations. Before having a baby, you spend time going to the movies, sleeping in, or just about anything you want. But once you have a baby, spontaneity will be hard to achieve, and you need to keep this in mind. You also won't be getting good sleep for a couple of months, no matter how great a sleeper your newborn is.

- **The "us" time.** Keep the love alive by making plans together. Having a baby doesn't mean you two won't be going out on your own. The newborn will definitely seek a lot of attention, but you just have to be intentional about spending time with your partner and planning things accordingly.

- **Talk to each other.** At the end of the day, talk to each other about all the things you have in mind. Talk about your expectations, your aspirations, or even mundane things like how you plan to divide the chores.

- **Family roles.** Talk about the family roles that both of you take in the family. People, by their very nature, take upon themselves certain roles. It varies based on how they interact and behave. For example, someone may be playing the role of a peacekeeper, reducing the tension in times of conflict.

- Right now, you and your partner are gearing up for your new roles—mom and dad. As you enjoy this phase, don't forget to be patient with yourself when you face emotional turmoil. Talk to each other openly about any feelings that you experience, even resentment. The next chapter talks about entering the second trimester and taking care of yourself along with the mom-to-be.

Chapter 4:

Month 4—Making Home

Homely

I feel like the success of parenthood is feeling like I failed all day today, but I get to wake up tomorrow and do it again and hopefully they turn out to be a good human being. —Justin Timberlake

There's no better news than expecting your first baby. When your partner tells you she's pregnant, you know that you have plenty of exciting times waiting for you ahead. However, at the same time, becoming a parent also means going through a lot of changes on an emotional level, so are you ready for that? Even if you aren't, don't worry because I've got your back. In this chapter, I'll first walk you through some of my personal tips that will assist you in preparing yourself emotionally, and then we'll move on to the changes that happen to your partner in the fourth month of pregnancy.

How to Prepare for Parenthood Emotionally

There are only a few experiences in life that can be compared to that of becoming a parent. With a newborn comes new stresses, new challenges, and new worries, but along with that also comes an immense amount of joy and happiness. Most people suggest that becoming a parent is the one job in this whole world for which anyone is least prepared. There will be several instances where you'll feel like you're failing, and in this section, we'll discuss how you can keep your ground in those instances and maintain your emotional balance.

- **Let go of realizing idealized parenthood.** Setting unrealistic expectations for parenthood never really works. There's nothing called a perfect parent; you should get that idea out of your head. On this parenthood journey, you'll make some mistakes, and trust me, it's no big deal. There's no need to be so hard on yourself. There will be some things that come easily to you, whereas other things might take some practice. What you need to do is try not to feel too stressed or overwhelmed.

- **Talk to your partner often and about everything.** Having an honest chat with your partner every now and then about your everyday life often helps. You don't have to talk about anything specific—just talk about whatever comes to your mind first. What is important is emotional support—it can work wonders when you both are going through such a tough time. You can talk about what you both did during the day, dividing chores around the house, doctor appointments, and so on.

- **You'll need recovery time from childbirth too, but not when your partner needs it.** Your partner has given birth to your child, but that doesn't mean you haven't done anything—you've also endured the emotional stress during the nine months, and you deserve a break too but not when your partner is going through her recovery time. Having the same recovery time is how conflicts arise, and you must avoid this as much as you can. But when you do need some time to cool off, remember that your friends and family are always there to provide you with the support you need.

- **Make time to sleep properly.** New parents are often sleep-deprived, and when you don't get sufficient sleep, you tend to become angrier, messy, nervous, and tense. So, try to get some sleep when your baby is sleeping. Take turns tending to the baby so that the other partner can sleep when one partner is taking care of the baby. Your sleep schedules may not match your previous ones but you have to ensure that you're squeezing in some good hours of sleep throughout the day.

- **Use social support to normalize your emotions.** Society often overlooks the mental health of fathers. Did you know that perinatal depression is common in 10% of fathers, and perinatal anxiety is seen in 15% of fathers (Darwin et al., 2021)? But then, society doesn't seem to understand that men are no different from women in terms of mental health—at the end of the day, they're just human beings. So, if you're struggling to normalize the emotions you're going through, make sure you seek social support.

- **Take out time for yourself, your friends, and your passions too.** Just because you're going to have a baby doesn't mean you'll forget all else. You're supporting your partner, going to your day job, and helping your partner around the house, but are you taking out time for yourself? I am guessing not because that seems to be the trend among most fathers. Please don't do that. Plan that day out with your friends. Go on that fishing trip, golf trip, or whatever you had planned. Watch a movie. Read a book. Do whatever makes your heart smile. Just don't forget to live.

It's only natural for first-time parents to spend more time in the "parent" role, but it's also equally important to take care of your emotional well-being. Now, let's move on to the changes that happen to your partner's body so that you're better prepared to take care of her.

Changes in the Mom

Apart from the regular symptoms like fatigue, nausea, mood swings, tender and swollen breasts, bloating, constipation, indigestion, heartburn, milky discharge from the vagina, etc., the following are the symptoms to watch out for in new mothers.

- **Colostrum, the first milk that mothers produce.** This is the time when a pregnant woman starts producing colostrum, also known as the first milk. This is marked by the breasts becoming bigger and veins becoming more visible. This is a sign that the milk duct system in your partner's body is becoming fully developed so that it can produce milk for the baby when it arrives (even if it arrives early).

- **Swollen and bleeding gums.** Almost 50% of pregnant women complain of bleeding gums, but do you know why? (Calton-Weekes, 2018). The gums usually bleed when they try to floss or brush their teeth. Women during this time suffer from a condition known as pregnancy gingivitis. The condition makes the teeth super sensitive to plaque and is mainly the result of the various hormonal changes occurring in their bodies. The effect can be minimized by practicing good oral hygiene.

- **Round ligament pains.** Women have ligaments on either side of their uterus whose main function is to thicken and stretch during the pregnancy phase to support the growing belly. When these ligaments undergo structural change, they cause what is known as round ligament pain. Once your partner has had an active day, the pain can feel like a dull ache. At other times, it can feel like a stabbing feeling in response to any movement. The pain is usually harmless, but if it's severe and lasts more than an hour, then you should call her healthcare provider as it can be a sign of placental abruption or severe preeclampsia.

- **Leg cramps.** Your partner's body is now carrying around extra weight all the time, and this leads to a change in the stress level on the leg muscles and also alters blood circulation. These two factors can lead to leg cramps. However, some experts are of the view that if the woman is deficient in calcium, it can cause cramps.

- **Feeling hot.** As I mentioned, a pregnant woman has much more blood flowing through her body than a normal woman. Hence, this makes her feel hot almost all the time. In order to handle the extra blood flowing through the veins, the blood vessels undergo slight dilation, and this brings the blood closer to the surface of the skin. This is the main reason why women feel hot during the second trimester. And if your partner is pregnant during the summer, they can most definitely feel toasty!

- **Darkened skin on the face or chloasma.** It's common among women to develop blotchy skin during their pregnancy. This is even more common in women who have a darker complexion. The condition has a specific term to it—melasma or chloasma. These skin changes will usually disappear on their own once you've undergone labor. The spots typically show up around the forehead, cheekbones, nose, and upper lip area. Women are more likely to develop this condition if it's in the family.

- **Increased appetite.** It's during the second trimester when your partner's pregnancy hunger will grow to its peak, and there's a good reason for it. They aren't only eating to support their own nutritional needs but also those of your baby. They need to support increased fat reserves, their growing breasts, and an increased blood volume. As a rule of thumb, it's said that women need to consume somewhere around 300–350 calories more than the usual amount at the beginning of the second trimester (Bellefonds, 2022).

- **Pregnancy glow.** Even though not every woman experiences the pregnancy glow, for those who do, it starts around the second trimester. This flushed look is mostly the result of hormones in your partner's body like hCG, progesterone, and estrogen. It's also because the woman's blood volume increases by almost 50% at this point (Pearson, 2017). The skin looks rosier because of more circulation of blood. The hormone fluctuations also lead to the production of more natural oils that cause this natural glow.

- **Back pain.** Back pain is a very common occurrence among women during pregnancy. This is because the abdominal muscles are weakened as the uterus expands in the body. This, in turn, puts excessive pressure on the lower back area. The hormonal changes that your partner is going through also relax the ligaments and joints around the pelvic area, causing pain and unsteadiness. Some activities that can reduce discomfort and strengthen the muscles are pelvic tilts, swimming, walking, prenatal yoga, and weight training. So, you must encourage your partner to do these.

- **Forgetfulness.** Moms-to-be have often reported forgetfulness and that they have trouble focusing, although researchers are still not sure why. It can be a combination of fatigue, anxiety, and stress. You can encourage your partner to use the different productivity and time management apps to keep track of their day if forgetfulness is hampering their day-to-day life.

- **Pregnancy headaches.** Cutting back on the caffeine, lack of proper sleep, dehydration, and stress—all of these things lead to pregnancy headaches, and let me tell you, women experience them quite often. However, don't waste time calling the doctor if your partner complains of a severe headache in the second trimester because it can indicate preeclampsia.

- **Snoring.** Do you know why women snore during pregnancy? Well, here, too, the hormones are to blame. The rise of progesterone and estrogen in the blood causes the mucus membranes inside the nose to become swollen. This means that your partner lies down, the congestion increases, and this makes them snore. Some experts also say that excessive weight gain during pregnancy for some women can also be the underlying cause.

- **Starting to show.** By now, your partner's tummy is out a tad bit, and she's starting to show. This experience can be quite the thrill because you and your partner can get a visible check of the baby you're eagerly waiting for.

This was a comprehensive list of all the changes a woman goes through during this month of her second trimester. In the next section, we'll take a closer look at baby development.

Changes in the Baby

By this time, your baby is quite grown. Its heart is already at work and pumping approximately 25 quarts of blood daily (Pevzner, 2021). As the baby keeps developing, this amount will keep on developing. The hair follicles have also formed on the baby's scalp, and these follicles are going to remain for the rest of its life. Let's take a detailed look at some of the other changes going on inside the womb.

Bone Formation

Until now, the fetus only had soft cartilage but now bone formation is taking place in your baby. The various genes dictate the basic outline for bones in your baby's body. Around the seventh week, the overall skeleton is already laid out with cartilage. To ensure proper development of the bones, your partner needs to intake sufficient levels of calcium and phosphorus. It's advisable that she takes it (Murray, 2021). If the food sources for calcium are insufficient, talk to the doctor for some prenatal supplements.

Placenta Growing Stronger and Thicker

The umbilical cord starts becoming stronger during this phase. It's the main lifeline of the baby as it connects to the placenta. By the time your partner reaches the end of her pregnancy, the umbilical cord will be approximately 1 in. thick and 20 in. long! (Scogna, 2021). The nutrients from the mother's body are transported into the baby through the umbilical cord and it's through the same pathway that waste is taken out of the baby.

Sweat Glands Are Developing

By the fourth month, the sweat glands of the baby have started developing. And in the next few weeks, all the layers of the skin will be fully developed. During the 13th week, the baby's skin is still thin but when the baby starts approaching the 16th week of the pregnancy, the skin starts to become thicker and sort of opaque. Taking a sufficient amount of Vitamin D is essential if you want healthy skin development for the baby.

How Can You Help?

With your partner being almost 17 weeks pregnant, you must be wondering about what are the different ways in which you can help them. Well, there are quite a few and the most important one of them at this stage is creating a birth plan. Let's take a look at your responsibilities one by one.

Help Them Sleep on Their Side

The second trimester can bring a lot of challenges to your partner's sleep. There's the problem of a stuffy nose and leg cramps, as mentioned in the previous section. Help your partner try out different sleeping positions. Get them a good quality pregnancy pillow because that often helps. Keeping the head in an elevated position and sleeping on the side also helps. When your partner sleeps on her back, it increases pressure on the blood vessels that are present on her back, reducing blood flow to the womb. According to experts, this increases the chances of stillbirth. Hence, sleeping on the side is always recommended.

Keep Them Moving

Many women are afraid of moving too much while they're pregnant, but some light exercises can actually help them gain the right amount of weight and also prepare them for labor. It can also help them sleep and feel better. You just have to ensure that she isn't engaging in activities that have low chances of a hard fall. One of the perfect things to do is walk. You can go on walks with your partner to keep them company. Walking three to five times a week for about thirty minutes should be enough for your partner to build strength and flexibility.

Help Them Deal With Tummy Touchers If They're Uncomfortable With Them

Is your partner tired of people being all touchy-feely with their baby bump? It's common among women, and not all mothers are comfortable with it. If your partner is unable to tell people not to touch her belly, you must have a stance prepared. So, if someone comes near her to touch her belly, your decision must be prepared, and you should be ready to politely say no to them and explain that she feels uncomfortable when anyone touches her belly. However, it's important that you're not snarky or rude about it.

Get Them New Undergarments

It's important that you invest in good-quality undergarments for your partner. You should avoid purchasing underwired bras because they can be quite uncomfortable for women during pregnancy, and most importantly, they can cause an obstruction in the growth of the breast tissue. Buy good quality maternity bras that have wide straps because these ensure that your partner's shoulders don't take all the burden. Also, get maternity shorts for your partner because they're super comfy when they're at home and also support the bump.

Talk About Birth Plans

Having a birth plan is essential, but just because you have one doesn't mean your delivery experience will be devoid of any surprises. The big day will be here before you know it, and so the fourth month is the perfect time to start working on the birth plan.

- **Do you have a birth plan?** A birth plan is exactly what the term suggests—it's a written plan in which everything ranging from your goals and wishes will be jotted down, not only before the delivery but also during and after labor and delivery. It will also include things that are practical and feasible and a list of your preferences.

- **Creating a birth plan.** Parents are usually tempted to include everything under the roof in a birth plan, but it's advisable that you keep it concise so that you can find the important details quickly when you need them. Some important things to note down are your partner's name, doctor's name, contact info, who you want to take with you when your partner gives birth, where your partner wants to give birth, pain meds, labor preferences, atmosphere, and so on.

- **Where do you want to give birth?** Moms-to-be are usually particular about the location of the birthing place. Some want to give birth in a hospital while some want to do it in a birthing center, and others want to do it at home. Keep in mind that most births happen in a hospital.

- **Labor room ideas.** Every woman has something in mind regarding their ideal labor room environment. Ask your partner what their preferences are and jot them down. They might want the lights to stay dim; some women want to try different positions while birthing the child, while others want to play their favorite music.

- **Who should be there?** No woman wants an unwanted visitor during labor. Ask your partner to specify who she wants in the labor room and note that down in the birth plan.

- **What do you need?** Note down all the things you would need during labor. For example, some women prefer a birthing chair while delivering the baby. If that is a requirement for you, note it down.

- **Pain medication or not?** You should clearly note down with your partner's consent whether she wants to take pain medications. This is because pain management is an integral part of labor. Some women know that they definitely want to be on an epidural while giving birth, and some know that they don't want it.

- **Postpartum options.** You should also note down important postpartum decisions that are commonly made, for example, umbilical cord blood donation, circumcision, rooming in, and so on.

Birth Plan Checklist for Husbands

Discuss with your partner and fill out this birth plan checklist.

Basic Information

- **Birth plan for:**

- **Partner's name:**

- **Hospital/birthing center:**

- **Due date:**

- **Doctor's name and contact info:**

Labor

- I don't want too many visitors during labor.

- I'd like to dim the lights.

- I'd like to play music.

- I'd like to wear my own clothes during labor.

- I'd like my partner to take photos or videos if the practitioner allows it.

- I'd prefer specific birthing positions.

- I'd like to eat if I wish to and if my practitioner allows it.

Pain relief

- Don't offer me an epidural right in the beginning.

- If my pain appears to be unbearable, only then offer an epidural.

- I don't prefer the word "pain" and rather want to use "comfort level" during labor.

Pushing

When it's time to push the baby out, I would prefer to:

- be told and coached on how and when to push

- push instinctively

- not be given any time limits as long as my baby and I are doing okay

The positions that I would like to try for pushing are:

- whatever feels right to me at that moment

- hands and knees

- squatting

- side-lying position

- semi-reclining

In case of a C-Section

- I'd prefer to be conscious if medically possible.

- I would want my partner to be by my side during the entire length of the operation.

- I want clear drapes so that I can see my baby as it emerges from me.

- I want to be able to breastfeed my baby in the recovery room.

- I want one arm to be left out of the cuffs so that I can hold the baby.

- As soon as the baby is dried, I want the baby to be given to my partner if it's appropriate.

Newborn care

- I want to meet my lactation consultant if possible.

- I want to hold the baby just after birth.

- I want to bank the umbilical cord blood.

- If possible, I want all the newborn procedures to take place in my or my partner's presence.

- I want 24-hour rooming-in with my baby.

- I want to keep the placenta and take it home.

- If my baby is a boy, I don't want circumcision performed.

- I want my baby to be given Vitamin K.

15-Week Pregnancy Checklist

When your partner is about 15 weeks pregnant, there are certain things that need to be done. Let's take a look at what you have on your plate.

- **Get them mentally prepared for amniocentesis and get it done. Be there for them.** Amniocentesis is a test that is done to check for any genetic disorders in the baby, for example, spina bifida or Down syndrome. A needle is inserted, and a sample of amniotic fluid is collected from the womb. The fluid is then tested to check for disorders. This prenatal testing is usually performed between the 15th and 20th week of pregnancy, and women can become anxious about getting tested. Hence, as the partner, you should be by their side offering emotional support.

- **Get them to keep a pregnancy journal.** Journaling is a good habit to maintain in any phase of life, and during pregnancy, a journal will keep you articulating every day's events in detail. One day, when your child grows up, you'll love sharing these notes with them; they will stay as a memory forever.

- **Make a second-trimester to-do list.** The second trimester is usually very busy because, amidst your partner's rapidly changing body, your energy is high planning for the baby's arrival. So, having a personalized to-do list helps maintain your mental calm because you know you have things under control. Note down everything you plan to do in the second trimester with your partner including things that are important for them during this phase.

- **Practice affirmations together.** Affirmations can do wonders to your mindset. It's very common for couples to get swayed into a negative mindset during pregnancy. So, it's important that you practice your affirmations together. These can be simple sentences like "I got this" or "I am strong, brave, and ready for a new family member." Say anything that makes you both feel positive.

- **Get them checked out at a dentist.** Hormonal changes put women at a greater risk of developing conditions like pregnancy gingivitis (we already discussed this earlier in the book). Hence, you should not neglect your partner's dental appointments just because she's pregnant.

- **Ask your older children to talk to the baby, give them time, and help them with their homework.**

This chapter was all about the fourth month of pregnancy which can be different for every woman, but overall, it brings you closer to the final day. Your partner is now in that phase when their regular clothes don't fit them that well and the maternity clothes are too loose. However, don't worry; you'll soon adjust to the change. The next chapter prepares dads for the fifth month of pregnancy.

Chapter 5:

Month 5—One Half Done.

One Half to Go!

I think [parenthood] brings out the child in all of us. That's what's so beautiful. It reminds you of the fascination you had with things, and how you can spend hours just being with someone. It's amazing. –Chris Hemsworth

Congratulations! You and your partner have reached the fifth month of pregnancy—this is when your partner may be literally feeling butterflies in her stomach. This process is also known as quickening. In this chapter, let's take a closer look at everything that goes on during this month and how you can support your partner throughout this time.

Changes in the Mom

Apart from the regular symptoms like fatigue, nausea, mood swings, and tender and swollen breasts, the following are the symptoms you should watch out for in new mothers.

- **Ravenous hunger.** When your partner is about 18 weeks pregnant, she'll be ravenously hungry almost all the time. She might even have some specific food cravings. It's important that you help her maximize her nutrition at this stage so that she can support the growing needs of the fetus. It's important to choose food items carefully. If you choose foods that are good in taste but offer no nutritional value, then they will add unnecessary weight. It's advisable that your partner tries six small meals throughout the day instead of having bigger ones. The focus should be on healthy fats, fibers, and proteins.

- **Dizziness because the changes in the cardiovascular system are too dramatic.** Your partner's cardiovascular and nervous systems are undergoing dramatic changes around this time, and it's quite natural for the body not to be able to keep up at times. This can sometimes make your partner feel dizzy or, worse, even faint. If they try to spring up too fast from a lying down or sitting position, the chances of dizziness increase further. You should let her healthcare provider know if the occurrence of dizziness increases in frequency.

- **Clumsiness.** When the baby bump finally starts to grow, many women feel clumsy. Their balance is off, especially when they try to do everyday things like climbing the stairs, carrying something, or walking on a slippery surface (they shouldn't be doing this anyway). Clumsiness also occurs as a result of pregnancy fatigue.

- **Breasts may have gone up a size.** As the estrogen levels keep rising during the second trimester, your partner's breast will feel fuller and might even go up in size. The main reason behind this is the development of the milk ducts. At this time, it's advisable that you buy a larger bra to accommodate the growth of their breasts.

- **Swollen hands and feet.** It's quite common and normal to witness swelling in your partner's hands and feet during this time of pregnancy. Their rings might be getting tight, and if that's the case, then it's advisable that they take them off. However, keep in mind that if the swelling is sudden and severe, there might be some serious underlying reasons, and you need to contact her healthcare provider immediately.

- **Thicker and shinier hair.** At around the 15th week of pregnancy, your partner may say that they have thicker and shinier hair than before. It's not that each hair strand has suddenly become thicker than before, but the growing phase of the hair cycle is longer than usual. In simpler terms, women face less hair fall. The scientific reason behind this is the rise in estrogen.

- **Lower abdominal pain.** Around week 19, your partner might experience lower abdominal cramping. However, if you notice that the cramping isn't going away on its own and is persisting for quite a while, it's time you call the doctor. Another warning sign is when pain radiates to the upper abdomen area.

- **Changes in their skin.** There are several skin changes that happen during pregnancy. Is your partner complaining that their palms are turning more red than usual? Well, there's nothing to worry about because this happens as a result of estrogen. They might also experience chloasma (explained previously in the book), whereby there are darkened patches on the skin. Another common change that you'll notice on your partner's skin is a dark line running from the pubic bone to the belly button—this is often referred to as the "dark line" or the linea nigra.

- **Belly button changes.** As the pregnancy progresses further, and your partner develops a baby bump, it might push the belly button to pop out. Several women complain that their belly button feels uncomfortable; however, rarely do they talk about belly button pain. If the belly button rubbing against your partner's clothing feels weird to them, ask them to wear loose-fitted clothes or cover the belly button with an adhesive bandage.

- **Leg cramps.** With the extra weight that your partner is carrying, leg cramps are common during pregnancy. Ask them to stretch their calf muscles whenever they feel uneasy. Apply a heating pad or give them a good massage for further relief.

This section comprehensively lists all the signs you should watch out for during the fifth month of pregnancy. In the next section, we'll discuss baby development in greater detail.

Changes in the Baby

Now that the pregnancy has progressed to the fifth month, your partner may start to feel the baby moving around in the womb. Some changes that happen at this stage are discussed below.

Ears in Final Positions

If you take your partner for an ultrasound at this point, you'll notice that the baby's nose, lips, and ears are all recognizable and developed—this is most definitely an exciting moment for you as parents. It was around the 12th week when the baby's ears had first developed specialized sound transmitters which are also known as hair cells. These hair cells are located inside the cochlea. After this, the hair cells form a connection to a nerve that further connects the ears to the brain and helps send sound impulses. This connection is made stable sometime around the 16th week, and this is also when the baby begins hearing faint sounds.

Lungs Starting to Branch Out

Now, let's talk about lung development. During the fifth month of pregnancy, small tubes known as bronchioles start to develop in the baby's lungs. Once they're developed, respiratory sacs start to appear at the end of these tubes. However, by the time your partner gives birth to the baby, tiny blood vessels will develop in the sacs, and they will further help in the exchange of oxygen and carbon dioxide in the lungs. It's because of these gaseous exchanges that the oxygenated blood is able to flow through all the blood vessels of the newborn.

Girl and Boy Parts All Set

At around 20 weeks, the baby's genitalia, bladder, and kidneys can be clearly captured in the ultrasound, which shows that these parts have developed at this point. For example, if your baby is a girl, then the fallopian tubes and uterus will have already formed by now. Similarly, if it's a boy, the ultrasound will be able to show its genitals. During this time, the testes of the baby begin the descent into the scrotum; however, the process isn't completed until late pregnancy.

Growth Spurt

Now that you've made it to the 20-week mark, your partner is literally halfway into the journey. Your little one weighs approximately 11.68 oz at this stage but owing to the growth spurt, your partner will start gaining weight more rapidly from this week (Miles, 2021a). Weight gain also depends on whether you're having twins and also on your partner's pre-pregnancy body mass index.

Taste Buds Can Transmit Signs to Brain

Your baby's taste buds are quite developed by now and did you know that they can even send signals to the brain at this stage? Yes, the food that your partner has eaten is passed on to the baby through the blood into the amniotic fluid. The food is in the form of molecules, and researchers are still not sure about whether or not babies can taste these molecules. However, there's some evidence from research that suggests whatever food your partner eats during the pregnancy stage plays some role in dictating the baby's taste later on in life (Getz, 2022).

Gallbladder Produces Bile

Sometime around the middle of the second trimester, the gallbladder can be seen for the first time in ultrasounds. But by the time your baby reaches the fifth month, the gallbladder is active, and it has started producing bile.

Fluttering Movements

As mentioned before, it's during the fifth month that your partner will feel the baby move for the first time. This is also termed *quickening*. For women who have been pregnant prior to this, quickening can happen a little earlier than this (sometime around the 16-week mark). But if your partner hasn't felt anything yet, there's no need to worry. You simply need to be patient now because not all pregnancies are the same, and for some, you may need to wait longer than usual.

Your little one has probably been moving in your womb for quite some time now, but it's only during the fifth month when the muscles are developed enough for your partner to feel those movements. But as the weeks progress further, your partner will be able to feel these fluttering movements in more pronounced ways.

Baby Brows

Your baby's skin is very smooth at this stage and extremely gorgeous (just like their future!) This is also the stage when your baby forms new eyebrows. Their skin is wrinkled yet translucent at this point in time. Because of the increased number of blood vessels in the body, the skin might appear red.

Hair on Their Head Getting Thicker

In the previous chapter, we had already talked about the formation of hair follicles. When baby development reaches the 20-week mark, downy hairs start to sprout from these follicles in areas like the chin, upper lip, and eyebrows. As time passes by, hair will slowly start to develop on the body of the fetus. At this stage, hair is referred to by a special term, lanugo. The main function of lanugo is to hold the vernix, which is a greasy substance that gives protection to the baby's skin as it's constantly exposed to the amniotic fluid in the womb.

Hearing Keeps on Improving

Your baby's hearing skills are much improved at this stage. They're able to hear faint sounds inside the body, including digestive sounds, heartbeat, and your partner's breathing. As the baby's hearing ability keeps improving, it will be able to hear these things more clearly with time. This is also why when your little one is born, it's advisable that you use a sound machine that mimics a whooshing sound that will make them feel they're still inside the womb and thus, help them sleep better.

Size Check

At 22 weeks, your baby is about the size of spaghetti squash and measures roughly 11.42 in. in length, and weighs 1.05 lb (Miles, 2021a).

How Can You Help?

There are several ways in which you can help your partner at this stage, and in this section, we'll discuss some of them.

Talk to Them About Kegel Exercises

Kegel exercises have a huge list of benefits. For starters, they help in preventing incontinence problems in women. Apart from that, they also help in a faster post-birth recovery and shorter labor. Sounds good, right? So, why not encourage your partner to do these?

When a woman has to push the baby out of her through the pelvis, it's a highly demanding job, and because of this process, the pelvic muscles of the woman have to stretch to new proportions. So, if you want your partner's pelvic muscles to work properly even after birth, then kegel exercises are extremely important. But what are Kegels? Well, these are exercises whereby you have to contract and relax the muscles of the pelvic floor for very short time periods. These exercises can also help with better bladder control and boost your partner's sexual health.

Help Them Continue Their Walks

It might not sound appealing to your partner that they have to move their body during pregnancy, but it's for their good health that they have to do this. It's even more important for women who are still experiencing morning sickness in their fifth month. According to the American College of Obstetricians and Gynecologists (ACOG) experts, moderate levels of exercise and walking during pregnancy can help lower the risk of preeclampsia, gestational diabetes, and the possibility of a C-section delivery. Some other benefits of walking include maintaining overall good cardiovascular health, improving the level of fitness, gaining only a healthy amount of weight, combating constipation, and so on. According to a 2009 review, women who went on walks while they were pregnant experienced a significant reduction in aches and pains, and their mood also improved (Olson et al., 2009).

Figuring Out the Gender of the Baby

One of the major pregnancy milestones is when you find out the gender of the baby. It's definitely a huge moment for both of you as parents. Around the 20th week, an anatomy scan is performed during the ultrasound when the baby's genitals and sex organs are fully developed. The baby's sex can be confirmed pretty easily unless and until your little one is in a position that makes it hard for the sonographer to tell. Accuracy levels are usually 97–99% and depend on the sonographer's experience.

- **Should you find out the sex of the baby?** This is a question that pops into most couples' minds when they're expecting a baby. These days, finding out the sex has kind of become the norm. People post pictures and videos of it on social media to the point that deciding not to find out the sex of the baby has become deviant. After all, why would you not want to know when technology is giving you this advantage? Well, it's not like that for all couples. So, you should not feel pressured by the expectations of society and only think about what you want as parents. It's completely okay to decide either way.

- **Pros and cons.** To give you some perspective, let's talk about the pros and cons of finding out the sex of the baby. The first and foremost advantage is that you can plan ahead. You can buy gender-specific things and even decorate the nursery accordingly. The name debates also become easier when you know the sex. Some people also believe that when parents know about the sex of the baby before, it helps in bonding. And last but not least, if you're not particularly good at being patient, you can always ask during the ultrasound scan what the sex of the baby is. Now, coming to the cons—well, these are fewer cons and more like pros of waiting to know the gender instead of knowing it before birth. First of all, there's the excitement of waiting till the last day. Secondly, if you're not too fond of buying too many blue or pink items, you get to buy non-gender-specific items. Then last but not least, you can avoid being disappointed because there's a slight chance of the baby's sex being predicted wrong, especially if it's in the wrong position.

- **Wardrobe preparation.** Preparing your baby's wardrobe is a huge task, and starting from the fifth month would be the right time. As expecting parents, this is also quite an exciting task to do together. Start with the basics. Since your newborn will mostly be sleeping or lying around, you need to choose soft fabrics that won't irritate their skin. You also need to get quick-access outfits since you'll frequently change their diapers during those first few months. I would like to bring to your notice that there's no hard and fast rule about how you set your baby's wardrobe, but some essential things that you should buy to get started are jumpers, pants, shirts, sleepers, hats, booties, and socks.

- **Room decor preparations.** The first thing to choose while deciding on the decor is a theme for your baby's room. Take your time because you don't want to choose a theme in a hurry that your baby will quickly outgrow in a few months or a couple of years. After that, you have to get the lighting, painting, and flooring done. The room should definitely be well-lit—that's non-negotiable. Once all of this is out of the way, it's time to buy the furniture. Some key essentials you need are a feeding chair, storage, a changing table, a bassinet, and a cot. You must also baby-proof the room, that is, there should be no sharp edges, and all electrical outlets should be properly covered. Moreover, for added safety, you should consider installing a baby monitor too.

- **Arranging the nursery.** This is another exciting part of the journey, but new parents often get carried away in the process. Hence, I'll provide you with some pointers that will help you stay on track and keep the essentials in mind. Invest in a good-quality cot and a mattress that will make your baby comfortable while they're sleeping. Some cots also come with drawers of their own, so that's quite a space-saving option if the room isn't so big. Choose black-out curtains—you'll thank me later when the summer sun doesn't wake your baby up. It's great to buy cute baby wardrobes, but I would suggest that if you have the space, then go for full-sized wardrobes because your baby is soon going to outgrow the baby wardrobe.

Let's hope this chapter was helpful in guiding you through the fifth month of pregnancy. There's definitely a lot to do now that the due date is coming closer. The next chapter marks the end of the second trimester and aims to prepare fathers for the rapid changes in the bodies of their partner, their needs, and how they can support them.

Chapter 6:

Month 6—Getting Second-

Trimester-Ready!

Do you have your finances arranged for the pregnancy? Have you made the necessary changes that you need to support your family? In this chapter, we'll learn the changes you need to make to have a smooth shift in case you need more than just paternity leave.

Changes in the Mom

When your partner is about 23 weeks pregnant, the baby starts getting more active and stronger. At this point, your partner will be able to easily tell that those aren't merely gas bubbles but baby kicks. Your partner should also feel warmer than before at this point. Let's take a detailed look at the changes that happen inside the body of the mother during the sixth month of pregnancy.

- **Swollen ankles.** Ankle swelling is quite common during this stage of pregnancy, and there are various factors that contribute to this. The first and foremost reason is that during this time, a woman's body retains a lot of fluid. Secondly, as the uterus grows in size, it starts putting additional pressure on the veins and this affects the process by which blood returns to the heart. Thirdly, hormones also play a role. You can advise your partner to wear compression stockings and be physically active as much as they can every day.

- **Swollen hands and face.** If you notice swelling in the hands and face of your partner, there's nothing to worry about because this is normal too. To meet the needs of the developing fetus, the female body has more blood and fluids, and this automatically causes swelling in other body parts. This extra swelling also prepares the female body for labor and delivery by opening up the pelvic joints and tissues. The extra fluids in the body of your partner are also responsible for the weight gained by your partner.

- **Their uterus grows.** The uterus grows to accommodate the growing baby, and by the end of your partner's second trimester, the uterus will have grown to the size of full-grown papaya. During this time, the size of the uterus is such that it no longer fits inside the cavity of the pelvis. It sits midway between the breasts and the navel. The uterus will also start generating pressure on the surrounding muscles and organs as it grows in size, causing mild pains, but this is completely normal and expected.

- **Weight gain.** Weight gain is normal during pregnancy, but the amount of weight a woman should gain varies from one person to the other. You can ask your partner's doctor about this, and they should be able to advise you regarding how much weight your partner should gain healthily. In general, it's said that a woman gains approximately 3–4 lb during the first trimester, after which she starts gaining 1 lb a week (Johnson, 2020). It's extremely important that you ensure your partner is gaining the right amount of weight because the mother's weight affects the baby's weight.

- **Pale skin? Check for anemia.** Do you think the natural blush on your partner's face has faded? Well, it happens to some pregnant women during this time. They might not look their best, and there could be a myriad of reasons at play, starting from an iron deficiency to general fatigue. However, anemia is usually one of the most common reasons why women look pale during pregnancy, especially towards the end of the second trimester. This is a condition when the red blood cells in your partner's body aren't able to transport sufficient oxygen to the various parts of the body. Pregnant women are more susceptible to developing anemia because, during this time, their flow of blood has increased, and they need much higher levels of folate and iron to keep up with the required levels of healthy red blood cells in the body. Some other common reasons behind the paleness include vomiting, inadequate sleep, and general fatigue, all of which are quite common during pregnancy. However, it's advisable that you get your partner checked for anemia just to rule it out.

- **Backache.** As the baby keeps growing, it can be quite tough on your partner's back. Most women complain of backache as they proceed towards the second half of pregnancy. The back pain usually originates at the sacroiliac joint, which is where the spine and pelvis bone meets (Dunkin, 2010). There are several reasons for this backache.

  o Firstly, in a healthy pregnancy, a typical woman will gain anywhere between 25 and 35 lb and that's a lot of weight for the spine to support all of a sudden (Johnson, 2020). This can cause lower back pain.

- o There's a change in the center of gravity when a woman is pregnant. A woman doesn't even notice how she begins changing her posture as the months progress resulting in strain on her spine.

- o Thirdly, the release of relaxin in the body during pregnancy is necessary for preparing the female body for the birthing process by loosening up the pelvic muscles. But the same hormone also causes instability of the spine and backache.

- o Fourthly, as the uterus keeps expanding to accommodate the growing baby, the rectus abdominis muscles which run parallelly from the rib cage all the way to the pubic bone might have a chance to get separated along the center seam. If that happens, your partner's back pain will worsen for obvious reasons.

- o Last but not least, women go through extreme emotional stress during this period which is also an additional factor for backache. Your partner might feel spasms in the back from the accumulation of tension in the region. If stress is the reason for backache, then you'll notice that the backache is worsening when your partner is too stressed.

- **Numbness or tingling.** This symptom is also the result of the uterus growing in size. When it grows, it puts pressure on the nerves present in your partner's legs. This might lead to a feeling of tingling and numbness in the toes and legs. It would feel as if someone is pricking the skin with pins and needles. There's no need to worry about these symptoms because it's completely normal and once you give birth, they will go away on their own in a few months. The same feeling can also be felt in your hands and fingers. It often triggers when your partner wakes up in the morning. For some, this feeling can be quite uncomfortable, and you can talk to their doctor about how to deal with the problem. Persistent numbing should be checked for any serious concern.

- **Hemorrhoids.** Hemorrhoids are more common in women who have a constipation problem during pregnancy. This is a condition whereby the veins in the rectal and anus region get swollen, and it can be very painful. The region might sting, itch, or even bleed, especially after or during bowel movements. However, the good news is that even though the condition is a painful one, it's short-lived.

- **Itching.** Your partner's skin stretches a lot during this stage as the belly becomes bigger and the breasts go up a size. If the itching is moderate, it's usually manageable and not a cause for concern. Some coping strategies include wearing loose-fitted clothes, applying lotion, and taking oatmeal baths. But if you see that your partner's itching is worsening or is converting into a rash, you need to let the doctor know immediately. Sometimes, this can be a sign of a pregnancy complication that goes by the name of cholestasis.

- **False labor (Braxton Hicks contractions).** Around the sixth month, your partner may experience false contractions, also known as false labor or Braxton Hicks contractions. These are irregular uterine contractions, and you need not be afraid of them because they're perfectly normal. This is simply the female body's way of preparing it for real labor. These contractions come like a tightening in the abdomen and then go away. They can be uncomfortable, and some women even say that they feel like mild menstrual cramps. However, something to keep in mind is that these contractions will never get too painful.

- **Sleeping difficulties.** It's quite unfair that when your partner's body needs to sleep the most, they seem to not get it. For some, insomnia during pregnancy is related to having crazy dreams while for others, it happens because of anxiety. Women also have to visit the bathroom quite frequently, which hampers their sleep. On top of that, some women face restless leg syndrome and leg cramps. Other than these, it's quite difficult to become comfortable with the growing belly, and that's another reason why women can't seem to fall asleep easily.

- **Swollen feet.** Moderate swelling in the feet is common during the sixth month of pregnancy. Approximately two-thirds of pregnant women face edema (accumulation of fluid in the tissues of the body that leads to swelling). Hormonal changes in the body are also responsible for the swelling. Some things that can help relieve the swelling include drinking sufficient water, wearing compression socks, and getting off your feet.

- **Restless legs.** Restless legs are characterized by a creepy crawly sensation in the lower legs to the point that women feel the need to move their legs even when they're resting. They get temporary relief when they move, which is what gives this problem the name restless leg syndrome. About 20% of pregnant women experience this problem (Sauer, 2022). The symptoms can be worsened by smoking and drinking caffeine.

- **Extra body hair.** We already spoke about thicker hair as a symptom of pregnancy in the previous chapter, but an addition to it is the change in the thickness of body hair as well. The hormone levels in your partner's body will cause a noticeable change in the overall hairiness. Some safe methods of removing body hair during pregnancy include threading, tweezing, shaving, and waxing.

Changes in the Baby

The baby has undergone huge developments by now. The little one has also started to inhale and exhale amniotic fluids in small amounts by the 26th week and this is an important phase for the development of its lungs. Let's take a detailed look at the other forms of development that are going on right now.

The Late Night Lovers, Active at Night

Do you know a funny thing about babies when they're inside the womb? They like to move around more when their mommies are lying down. Yes, and this is the reason behind babies being more active at night, which also adds to insomnia in pregnant women. When your partner is up and about all day long, the baby is mostly asleep because they're lulled to a sleep-like state by all the movement that is happening. The moment the woman slows down to rest, the baby wakes up.

Testicles Begin to Descend

If your baby is a boy, then around the sixth month, his testicles will begin descending into the scrotum. This trip isn't finished in a day or two or even a week—it takes approximately two to three months for the testicles to fully descend. However, in some cases, an abnormality happens, and this descent of testicles doesn't happen. In that case, the baby is born with either one or both of his testicles undescended, and in most of these cases, the babies undergo a premature birth.

Distinct Sleep-Wake Pattern

With the development of the pregnancy, your partner will notice that the baby is developing a certain sleep-wake pattern inside the womb. For example, your little one might wake you up every morning with kicks and flutters, or they might be more active during the evening when you're cuddling with your partner. Babies are asleep most of the time while they're inside the womb. In fact, according to research, they spend 90% of their time sleeping by the time the pregnancy reaches 38 or 40 weeks (Poblano et al., 2008).

Eyelids Open

By the 27th week, your baby can now open and close its eyes. They can even move in response to light. For example, if you flash a bright light at your tummy, you might feel the intensity of kicks increase. If you want to support the good vision for your baby, make your partner intake sufficient amounts of beta-carotene. It's present in abundant amounts in red, orange, and yellow vegetables and fruits, and some examples include squash, sweet potatoes, and carrots. Keep in mind that you don't need to give your partner too much retinol while she's pregnant, even though retinol is known to be good for the eyes. This is because when taken in high doses, it can cause liver toxicity and birth defects.

Hiccups

If your partner is experiencing small yet rhythmic movements in the womb, then they're likely to be fetal hiccups. One episode of fetal hiccups can last for a few moments, and there's nothing to worry about because this, too, is completely normal. The sensation might be strange so ask your partner to sit back and relax. Now, if you're wondering why babies get hiccups when they're inside the womb, well, that is a question even researchers are trying to find the answer to, but one theory states that by doing this, the baby tries to regulate the amniotic sac fluid in its own way.

Size Check

By this time, your baby is almost the size of a cauliflower measuring approximately 14.5 in. in length and having a weight of 2.33 lb (Miles, 2021a).

How Can You Help?

Now that your partner is nearing the third trimester, the doctor visits will increase in frequency—it can be every two weeks or even weekly. This is a prime time for you to be with her and cater to her needs. I've spoken about prenatal visits in the previous chapters, and the later ones aren't going to be any different. The only difference is that your partner might have to undergo some more tests and ultrasounds. Some ways in which you can help her are as follows.

Buy Them New Shoes

I've mentioned time and again how pregnancy leads to increased water retention in the female body and this makes it necessary for your partner to buy new shoes. Their feet will ache and swell more than ever, and you need to make sure you're doing everything you can to make them feel comfortable. Another common issue of the legs during pregnancy is varicose veins, whereby the veins grow in size due to the increased pressure on them from the growing uterus. Exercising and walking while wearing the right shoes will help regulate blood flow. Women also experience heel pain during pregnancy. This happens because there's a shift in the balance of the body, and if your partner is standing for long hours wearing the wrong shoes, it can cause heel pain.

Preterm Labor Preparations

Women often know if they're going to have a premature baby. In those cases, it helps if you're prepared for the process. Before we go into the details of preterm labor preparations, let me explain to you what preterm labor is. Any typical pregnancy has a length of approximately 40 weeks. But when labor starts before reaching the mark of the 37th week of pregnancy, it's known as premature labor. Premature labor does not always mean premature birth. You need to consult your doctor regarding this.

- **Tests and procedures.** In order to diagnose preterm labor, there are certain tests and procedures that can be done, which include the following.

  - o *Pelvic exam:* The tenderness/firmness of the uterus along with the position and size of the baby can tell whether your partner is going into preterm labor. The placenta won't cover the cervix if the water has not broken yet. Hence, a cervix exam can determine whether the cervix is open. The healthcare provider will also check for any potential bleeding from the uterus.

- ○ *Uterine monitoring:* A uterine monitor is used to measure the spacing and duration of the contractions.

- ○ *Ultrasound:* A transvaginal ultrasound will be done, and this will help in measuring the length of the cervix. It will also help in figuring out the volume of the amniotic fluid, confirm the position of the baby and problems of the placenta, and give an estimation of the baby's weight.

- ○ *Lab tests:* Certain lab tests of your partner's vaginal secretions will be done to check if it contains fetal fibronectin or any sign of infection. The former is a substance that is released during labor.

- **Treatment.** The treatment options for preterm labor are as follows.

- ○ *Medications:* Once a woman is in labor, no surgery or medication can stop it, but certain medications might be prescribed by the doctor for other purposes. If your partner is between 23 and 34 weeks pregnant and has a chance of premature delivery in the next 7 days or so, the doctor might prescribe corticosteroids for the lung maturity of the baby. If your partner is between 24 and 32 weeks of pregnancy and is going into preterm labor, the doctor might prescribe magnesium sulfate as some research shows it reduces the chances of cerebral palsy for babies. The doctor might also give your partner a dosage of tocolytic that helps in slowing down the contractions.

○ **Surgical procedures:** If your partner has a short cervix and is having preterm labor because of that, then a procedure termed cervical cerclage might be followed. Here, the cervix is closed with the help of stitches and then removed once 36 weeks of pregnancy are completed.

○ **Preventive medication:** If your partner has a history of preterm labor, preventive medications in the form of weekly shots of progesterone might be provided by the doctor. Progesterone might be directly inserted into the vagina, which prevents preterm birth.

• **Coping and support.** Women usually feel anxious when they come to know that they're at risk for preterm labor. You should always be by their side during this phase and give them emotional support. You should also consult your doctor and find healthy ways of relaxation for your partner.

For the Baby

Let's take a look at the different processes that happen with the baby when they're born prematurely.

• **Possible tests.** Some possible tests that might be done on your premature baby include the following.

o **Blood tests:** A needle or a heel stick is used to collect the blood sample, which is then used to check for some critical substances like glucose, calcium, and bilirubin levels. The red blood cell count is also checked to see if there's any chance of infection or if the baby is suffering from anemia.

o **Breathing and heart rate monitor:** The heart rate and breathing of your baby will be monitored day and night. Apart from that, blood pressure readings will also be taken at regular intervals.

o **Echocardiogram:** This test will reveal whether the baby's heart is functioning properly.

o **Fluid input and output:** The neonatal intensive care unit (NICU) team will thoroughly maintain a chart of how much fluid the baby is taking in and how much fluid it's losing through wet and soiled diapers.

o **Ultrasound scan:** This scan will be done on the brain to see if there's any fluid buildup or bleeding. It will also be done on the organs of the abdominal region.

o **Eye exam:** An ophthalmologist will be called to check for problems with the retina and vision.

- **Treatment:** Round-the-clock care will be provided to the baby by the NICU team.

o **Supportive care:** Specialized supportive care is offered to premature babies. Your baby will be placed in an incubator so that normal body temperature can be maintained. After that, the staff will show you how to hold the baby with skin-to-skin contact, also known as "kangaroo care." Some sensors will be attached to the baby's body with tapes that will monitor essential things like temperature, breathing, heart rate, and blood pressure. In the beginning, you cannot feed the baby directly. Hence, an intravenous tube will be attached through which fluids and nutrients will be sent into the baby's body. If the baby has jaundice, it will be placed under bilirubin lights. If the blood volume of the baby isn't enough, they might also need a blood transfusion.

o **Medications:** In order to ensure normal functioning of the lungs and to promote maturing of the baby, certain medications will be given. However, the type of medications will depend on your baby's current condition. For example, if your baby is suffering from respiratory distress syndrome, surfactant might be given. Similarly, certain medications are given to manage urine output and control excess fluid. On the other hand, if there's a risk of infection, antibiotics will be prescribed.

o **Surgery:** Sometimes, certain critical conditions associated with prematurity need to be treated with surgery. The baby's healthcare team will be able to help you out regarding this. You have to talk to them regarding which surgery would be the best and what would be the best course of action.

Check Up on Yourself

Caretakers need to be taken care of too. Becoming a dad isn't easy. You're juggling so many roles—you're a husband, you have work, and now you're wrapping your head around the fact that you're a soon-to-be-dad. You need to understand that these relationship changes are normal, and you need to get accustomed to these changes, but at the same time, you should check up on yourself from time to time.

- **Analyze how you're doing.** For some men, getting the news that you're going to have a baby can bring mixed feelings, and that's completely okay. You don't always have to put on a happy face if you don't feel like it. You could feel numbness, shock, anxiety, or even panic. Everyone needs time to adjust. Eventually, most men get there, but it all starts feeling real only after the baby is born. You should analyze your feelings from time to time and accept your feelings rather than trying to "fix" them. If you're feeling left out of the pregnancy, bring it up with your partner and discuss how you can become more involved.

- **Are you financially solid?** One of the important parts of preparing for the baby is preparing your finances. Financial stability is crucial for every expectant parent. According to a USDA report from 2017, an average American couple belonging to the middle class spends approximately $296,684 on raising a child up to the age of 18 right from birth (Batcha & Srinivasan, 2021). Below are some tips to keep in mind to get your finances ready before the baby arrives.

    o *Reduce your credit card debt:* Start with your credit cards. Don't add new expenses, especially the ones you don't need. You can also consider transferring the balance amount to a credit card that charges a lower amount of interest.

o **_Keep track of your spending:_** Carefully track where you're spending your money. This will help you determine where you can reduce your spending. Keep notes on your phone and go paperless. This will reduce the hassle.

o **_Practice austerity:_** It's time to curb that good life for a while until the baby comes. Remember, a lot of money is already going to go towards buying baby gear.

o **_Purchase life insurance:_** Expectant parents should consider buying life insurance that is about 6–8 times their gross annual salary.

o **_Create a will:_** Even if you think it's too early, trust me, it's not. It's wiser to choose a guardian for your child who will manage the finances in case both parents die.

o **_Don't forget your retirement:_** Amidst all this chaos about being financially solid for your newborn, you cannot afford not to put some money aside for your retirement—it should always be prioritized.

- **Have you worked out your leave and holidays?** You must take your paternity leave and help out your partner because this is the time you have to be with her. It has also been seen that pregnant women whose partners take leave during this phase have a lesser tendency to go into depression.

- **Are you well-rested?** When you get involved in taking care of your partner, there will be times when you yourself will also feel tired and exhausted. Hence, it's important that you take the necessary rest.

If you haven't taken your leave yet, figure out a healthy work-life balance. Don't take too much on yourself; otherwise, you'll face burnout, which won't benefit anybody. Now that we have covered everything related to the sixth month, we'll move on to the next chapter, which prepares fathers for the seventh month of pregnancy.

Chapter 7:

Month 7—The Trials of the Third Trimester

My children's happiness, their safety, and their well-being, is the most paramount thing in my life. You just want to protect them at all costs. –
John Krasinski

Now that your partner is seven months pregnant, the baby has started to look almost like the way you'll soon meet it after delivery. For example, the skin is becoming less transparent, and the overall body is plumping up. There are certain physical changes in the face, and all of this is making your partner's belly grow more. In this chapter, -we'll first have a look at the changes that your partner will have to undergo during this month, and then move on to the changes in the baby.

Changes in the Mom

Apart from the regular symptoms that have already been discussed several times in this book, like tender and swollen breasts, mood swings, nausea, fatigue, and so on, the following are the other symptoms to watch out for in new mothers.

- **Baby kicks.** Baby movements inside the womb continue to change throughout the pregnancy. It's never the same. But once you've started to enter the third trimester, the baby kicks will start to intensify, and they will happen every day! The womb might be confined for the baby; despite that, they make a lot of movement. In fact, some research also suggests that by the time a woman reaches 30 weeks, a baby can generate up to almost 10.5 lb of force (Frothingham, 2020).

- **Leg cramps.** Apart from varicose veins and swelling, women also experience leg cramps. They're a very uncomfortable part of pregnancy. These cramps are sharp and sudden pain that occurs in the feet and calf muscles. The cramps mostly occur at night and are a sign that the muscles are undergoing a strong contraction when they shouldn't. When your partner is undergoing a leg cramp, it's common for them to become confused and not know what to do. Moderate and regular exercise during pregnancy can help relieve these leg cramps. But you should let your partner's doctor know if the cramps are too painful and are frequently happening or if they aren't letting them sleep.

- **Nail changes.** With the sudden influx of hormones in the female body, you might notice that your partner's nails are growing faster than ever before. Don't be surprised if you notice that your partner has long nails all of a sudden. Some women might suffer from grave issues, too, like thickening of nails, detachment, ingrown nails, brittleness, splitting, and white lines or dots.

- **Gas and bloating.** You've already heard about progesterone and its various functions throughout the female body. One of its functions is relaxing the muscles not only in the pelvic area but throughout the body, which includes the gastrointestinal tract too. Now, you have to understand that your partner's abdominal region is already becoming crowded. This crowding, coupled with the relaxing of the muscles, has a direct effect on digestion and slows it down. When the digestion process becomes sluggish, it causes heartburn and gas. This happens, even more, when your partner has had a big meal. All of this, in turn, can lead to constipation.

- **Hemorrhoids.** Since the uterus is growing in size, there's a chance that it will contribute to hemorrhoids. As mentioned in the previous chapter, these are swollen blood vessels that occur in the rectal area, and these are quite common during this phase. However, the good thing is that once your partner has given birth, these usually clear up.

- **Light-headedness.** Light-headedness is experienced by some women during this time of pregnancy, and it's known as supine hypotensive syndrome. This usually happens when your partner is lying down flat on their back, and when they try to change their position, they feel dizzy. This is because of a sudden change in blood pressure and heart rate. The same can also be experienced if they stand up too quickly.

- **Fatigue.** Fatigue is the one symptom that will be by your partner's side throughout the pregnancy and not just in the third trimester. Some causes of fatigue include the following.

  o *Gestational diabetes:* Here, the woman's body becomes resistant to the insulin hormone, and a general sign of this is fatigue.

- o *Anemia:* Anemia is very common in pregnant women, especially after the 20th week when there's a drastic increase in blood volume, and this can take a hit on the iron reserves of the body of the mother. Lightheadedness/fainting coupled with fatigue is usually a sign of anemia.

- o *Thyroid problems:* The imbalance of the thyroid hormone in the body whereby either too little of it is present (hypothyroidism) or too much of it is present (hyperthyroidism)—both can lead to fatigue as a symptom.

- o *Prenatal depression:* If your partner seems to be more tired than usual and looks unusually sad, then they might be going through prenatal depression. Some other symptoms include wanting to sleep all the time, not wanting to sleep at all, apathy, and not wanting to eat. Remember, depression doesn't only affect the mother but also the baby.

- o *Chronic fatigue syndrome:* In rare cases, if the mother of your baby is facing extreme fatigue, the underlying cause might be chronic fatigue syndrome. Sometimes, it's also linked to a type of morning sickness that is very serious, also termed hyperemesis gravidarum.

- **Growing feet.** Are your partner's shoes no longer fitting them the way they did before? When your partner enters the third trimester, swollen feet become an added problem, and there are several reasons why this happens. The first reason is weight gain. When your partner gains weight, it puts extra pressure on their feet, causing them to flatten and become bigger in size. Secondly, hormonal changes also play a big role. The hormone relaxin relaxes the ligaments in your body, and since the bones in your feet aren't growing, the feet appear expanded or swollen even up to half a size more.

- **Mood swings.** The third trimester brings a lot of mood swings because your partner is anxious about the birthing process. They could fear that it's going to be too painful or that it will be an emergency C-section. These worries are all valid and normal. Your role is to support your partner throughout and make them feel that they aren't alone in this journey. With the hormonal change happening in their body, you might find them crying all of a sudden out of nowhere. Random crying is a common occurrence not only in the third trimester but throughout the pregnancy.

- **Managing labor pain.** They call it labor for a reason. Having a baby isn't an easy task. A woman has to go through a lot of hard work to give birth to a baby and a crucial part of that process is enduring the pain. From the seventh month onwards, your partner should start practicing the different ways of managing labor pain so that it's easier for them later on.

    o *Relaxation:* Relaxing the mind is the first step to managing the pain. When a woman lets fear take over, the pain becomes worse. Ask your partner to stay in the moment as much as they can and not think about labor.

    o *Breathing:* A great way to stay relaxed is to focus on breathing patterns. Whether your partner is inhaling deeply or panting, you must ask them to focus on their breaths until the pain starts to fade.

o *Move around:* Rolling around, changing positions, and walking often help to ease the labor pain. Being hooked in one place never really helps.

o *Massage:* Many people underestimate the role of massage in easing labor pain. But if you massage your partner's hands or rub their feet, it's going to provide them relief.

- **Braxton Hicks contractions.** The Braxton Hicks contractions will continue in the seventh month of pregnancy in a more pronounced manner than in the previous month. In fact, as the pregnancy progresses, these contractions will become more and more prominent. These will feel like a tightening around your partner's uterine muscles and they usually occur after an interval of 20 minutes or so.

- **Leaky breasts.** Some women might notice leaking from their breasts around this time, and there's nothing to be worried about because this is completely normal. Before your partner is due to have your baby, the breasts start to produce milk. The substance coming out of the leaking nipples is colostrum or the first milk. This is just a sign that your breasts are preparing to feed the baby. If the leaking is too much and it's bothering your partner, then you can ask them to wear absorbent breast pads.

Changes in the Baby

Reaching the seventh month is indeed a big milestone. But at the same time, keep in mind that the third trimester is going to be the most trying for your partner. The baby is the most active and the body is growing, both of which will take a toll on her. So, let's briefly have a look at all the changes happening inside the womb.

Strengthening Bones

The baby's bones are hardening, and in the meantime, they're soaking in a lot of calcium which helps in increasing their strength. You must encourage your partner to drink sufficient milk. If they aren't so fond of milk, then you have to find some alternative source of calcium like enriched orange juice, yogurt, or cheese.

Immature Lungs

You already know in the previous months that your baby's lungs have branched. Now, at the tip of those branches, there are respiratory sacs. These sacs have now begun producing a substance called surfactant. The main purpose of surfactant is to keep the lungs inflated even when the baby is exhaling or at any other time when there isn't sufficient air inside the lungs. The lungs have not fully matured in the seventh month, but if sufficient medical help is provided, they would be able to function, which is how premature babies survive.

Making Melanin

The 30th week marks a special week in baby development because this is when the skin cells of your baby start making melanin. Melanin will be responsible for giving your baby its skin color. As a rule of thumb, the more melanin, the darker the color of your baby's skin and hair. Melanin also protects your babies from sun exposure once they're born—protection they don't need when they're inside the womb. It's only after birth that melanin production increases, darkening the skin and giving your baby its actual skin complexion.

Amniotic Fluid Cushion

Your baby is surrounded by approximately a pint and a half of amniotic fluid, and between 34 to 36 weeks, the number of fluid peaks inside the womb. During this time, it averages at about 800 ml (MedlinePlus, n.d.). The baby keeps swallowing the fluid and also eventually releases it, so the amniotic fluid is never stagnant. It has a lot of functions, some of which include:

- It aids in the movement of the baby inside the womb, which, in turn, helps in better growth of bones

- It also helps in the proper development of the lungs

- It does not allow heat loss as it maintains a constant temperature for the baby inside the womb

- It does not allow excess pressure on the umbilical cord

- It acts as a cushion for the baby, protecting it from outside blows or any sudden movements.

Ability to See in the Dark

By the 30th week, the baby gains the ability to see through dim light and understand shapes. The pupils are now able to constrict and expand which gives the eyes the ability to decide how much light they will allow to enter. At this point, the baby's eyes have more rods than it has cones, and this is the reason why it's able to make out the outlines of objects but isn't able to detect the colors. At around the 31st week, the baby gains the ability to blink when exposed to bright light. For example, if you flash a bright light at your partner's tummy, she might experience some flutters and wiggles, which is nothing but the baby blinking in response.

Fattening Up

By the 31st week, your baby can now move its head from side to side. Their body, legs, and arms are also plumping up because fat accumulation has started. This extra accumulation of fat will also aid in smoothening out the wrinkles on the body of the baby. They will have chubby toes and chubby cheeks. During these weeks, every week is important. With each week that the baby is spending in the uterus, the chances of a preterm baby are lessening. Every preterm baby requires extremely special care in the NICU, but at 33 weeks, the chances of survival are almost definite.

Moving a Lot

By now, your baby is probably doing a lot of movement, and that is completely normal and even expected. They might be kicking and punching a lot which would cause sleeping problems for your partner. But you have to find comfort in the fact that all this movement means that your baby is active and healthy and there's nothing wrong with them.

Size Check

Your baby is approximately the size of a coconut now, with a length of 16.46 in. from head to toe, and weighing about 3.86 lb (Miles, 2021a).

Now that you've reached the seventh month, there will be a lot of decisions that you need to make, from what clothes you need to buy to which car seat you want to choose, and alongside everything, everyone around you will make a lot of opinions regarding what should be done. But remember, not all of them will be helpful. So, always do your own research before blindly trusting anyone.

How Can You Help?

With just a few weeks remaining before the due date, your responsibilities as the partner become even more important. By now, you've probably become a pro at understanding the female body, and in this section, we'll discuss how you can be of help to your better half in this seventh month of pregnancy.

Tour the Hospital or Birth Center You Have Chosen

Once you and your partner have narrowed down the hospital or the birth center where she'll give birth, you must visit the place. On tour, you'll get the opportunity to visit the recovery as well as the labor rooms. You'll also get an idea of their overall policies. You must ask whether you should pre-register your partner before the delivery or whether they have an option like that. You should also ask about all the paperwork that needs to be completed before admission and whether all that can be completed before labor. You should also ask about the comfort measures that the center or hospital encourages—whether they have access to birth balls, music, and stuff like that. Also, enquire about the visitor policies in labor rooms and what policies they have regarding siblings. You must also ask about the average length of stay, both in case of vaginal birth and a C-section. If you have any other questions in mind, jot them down before the tour, and make sure you have all your doubts cleared.

Meet With the Doula

Before you go for your meeting with the doula, take some time to sit down with your partner and write down all the questions that you have in mind. Whether your aim is to help your partner get a more empowering birthing experience or something else, having the questions with you beforehand makes the meeting smoother. It will help you communicate freely.

During the visit, the doula will examine your partner's medical and pregnancy history and also ask some questions about your lifestyle and family. The answers to these questions will help the doula cater to your partner's needs. The doula can also help you create a birth plan. She will work with you to ensure that your partner's birthing experience is exactly what she imagined it to be. The doula will make her feel confident, well-informed, and nurtured by providing her with continuous support and credible information. Apart from preparing your partner for birth, the doula will also help her with relaxation and peace during the pregnancy, right up to the delivery day.

Schedule an Appointment With the Caretaker

Choosing your partner's caretaker is yet another important step in the seventh month. You probably won't always be free as you have other things to do unless you get paternity leave. Even then, having someone else to solely look after your partner is always better than taking everything on your own shoulders. When you schedule an appointment with the caretaker, you must have your questions ready. You should ensure that the caretaker knows the basic things like what each procedure or test related to pregnancy means or what to do in case of an emergency situation. You should also ask them a little about their approach to pregnancy and see whether you both are on the same page.

How Are They Feeling?

It's a good bet that by now, your partner is quite anxious because most women are apprehensive about the delivery process, especially if it's their first pregnancy. With the uterus becoming bigger and bigger, they already feel stuffed and out of breath, and the anxiety only adds to it. Irrespective of whether the pregnancy was planned or unplanned, your partner might sometimes be happy, and they might quickly shift to a worried or anxious state, thinking, "Am I doing something wrong?" It's common for women to worry whether their baby will be okay at this stage. And if it's their first baby, they will obviously want constant reassurance that everything is going to be just fine. Make sure you provide her with that. You must ensure that she isn't too hard on herself because the internet will bombard her with images of happy mothers, and she'll be quick to compare herself with those images of women in glossy magazines. You have to be there for her in case she develops body image issues. Whatever she's feeling or going through, ask her to share it with you.

Make a Support Plan

The seventh month is the perfect time to chalk up a support plan. Sometimes, your close ones offer to pitch in once the baby is born. In that case, having a support plan is necessary if you don't want everything to fall into chaos. The support plan should clearly state what task you're allocating to which person. For example, someone might be responsible for buying meds; another person might be bringing meals on time, and so on. If you're too busy to make the plan, you can ask a friend to coordinate the support plan for you.

Click Pictures of the Baby Bump

Clicking baby bump pictures is one of the best ways to document your pregnancy. The seventh month is the best time to take these maternity photos because the bump is of the right size, and your partner isn't too late to go out and about. It won't be too taxing for them to get a photoshoot done during this phase. At the same time, it's late enough in the pregnancy period for your partner to show that perfectly round baby bump. Don't forget to moisturize your partner's belly for the best outlook. Get them a beautiful dress in which they would feel comfortable moving around. Avoid solid prints because they can be distracting. While the seventh month is the perfect time for maternity shoots, if you have multiple deliveries or have a high-risk pregnancy, you should get the shoot done earlier on.

Multiple Pregnancies? Get Ready for Them

It's a multiple birth if your partner is pregnant with twins or triplets, etc. As more and more women are opting for fertility treatments, multiple pregnancies are becoming quite common these days. But with multiple pregnancies comes the risk of fetal growth restriction, preeclampsia, and premature birth. In this section, we'll explore multiple pregnancies in a bit more detail to help you understand the intricacies.

- **Fraternal twins or identical twins?** Fraternal twins occur when two separate eggs are fertilized and then implanted in the same uterus. These twins can either look the same or different and can be of any gender. Each baby has its own amniotic sac and placenta and thus fraternal twins are considered to have the lowest risk among multiple pregnancies. On the other hand, identical twins are formed from a single fertilized egg. This egg splits in half to give rise to the twins. The babies formed from such an egg share the same DNA since each half is genetically identical. Identical twins may or may not share the same amniotic sac and placenta. They usually have several similar characteristics including facial features, but owing to environmental factors, identical twins might, later on, grow to look different.

- **Triplets?** Triplets are also categorized under higher-order multiples (HOMs). They can be a combination of identical and fraternal twins.

- **What increases the chances of multiple births?** There isn't one but several factors that increase the chances. If your partner is older, that is 30 or above, then there's a higher chance of multiple pregnancies. Other than that, if your partner is using a fertility drug or is a twin herself, or has twins in the family, then there's also a chance of multiple pregnancies.

- **How common are multiple births?** Multiple births are becoming more and more common in recent years, and this is because of fertility treatments and their rise in popularity. Procedures like IVF have a role to play in conceiving twins or triplets.

- **Signs of multiple pregnancies.** Performing an ultrasound exam is the only way you can know whether you're having multiple pregnancies or not. Some other signs include rapid weight gain especially in the first trimester, extreme nausea, more than usual amounts of protein alpha-fetoprotein in the blood, and high hCG levels. However, all these won't be a 100% sure diagnosis of multiple pregnancies until and unless you perform the ultrasound scan where the doctor will scan the inside of your partner's uterus.

- **Complications.** Irrespective of the number of babies your partner is carrying, complications can arise in pregnancy. But, with an increase in the number of babies, complications increase. Some possible complications linked with multiple births include gestational hypertension, premature birth and labor, placenta abruption, gestational diabetes, and fetal growth restriction.

As you're inching closer to the delivery date, time may feel like it's speeding up and slowing down simultaneously. Remind your partner to listen to their body and take cues as to when to power through and when to slow down. I hope this chapter was helpful to prepare you for the trying third trimester. The next chapter talks about the eighth month of pregnancy.

Chapter 8:

Month 8—Baby's Almost Here!

The nature of fatherhood is that you're doing something that you're unqualified to do, and then you become qualified when you do it. –John Green

When your partner is 32 weeks pregnant, it's highly likely that the baby has already turned head-down in the uterus. This is how it prepares for birth. During this time, the baby also becomes pro at regulating its body temperature. This is also something they need to become acclimated to their life outside of the womb. However, now that the baby has less room to move around, your partner may feel more discomfort. Let's take a look at all the things that go about during the eighth month of pregnancy so that you're better prepared for all the things that lie ahead.

Changes in the Mom

The baby is now close to maxing out the available space inside the uterus and thus, the eighth month is very significant in terms of change in the way the baby moves. Symptoms related to your partner's belly may also get worse. Here is a list of the symptoms you should look out for.

- **Kicking baby.** In the last few weeks, you probably had a hyperactive child where you even had to face a handful of bold kicks, but now, you'll notice that those kicks are getting replaced with nudges, knocks, squirms, and wiggles and all of this happens because of the reduced space in the uterus. But if you notice a drastic reduction in the activity of your baby and the daily kick counts, you should let your partner's doctor know right away.

- **Shortness of breath.** By the eighth month, the uterus has grown to such a size that it has begun pressing on the diaphragm. The diaphragm is the flat muscle in the body that moves when you breathe. Since the uterus presses against the diaphragm, the lungs are unable to fully expand the way they should. This ultimately leads to shortness of breath in women or shallow breathing.

- **Lower back pain.** Your partner's body is going through further changes to prepare for childbirth. As explained before, this leads to the loosening up of the connective tissues. The loosening up is important because it improves the flexibility of the pelvis, which, in turn, helps the baby to come out. However, a direct impact of this loosening is lower back and hip pain. This pain also occurs as your partner's posture changes, and they tend to lean forwards. This pain is often relieved when a woman sleeps on her side with a pillow in between her legs.

- **Trouble sleeping.** Everyone will keep telling their partner to get good sleep, and this will be the time she won't be able to get quality sleep. There's nothing more frustrating than this. There are several reasons behind this, like:

  o In the third trimester, your partner's uterus has become bigger in size and is pushing down on their bladder, which increases their trips to the bathroom. This increased urge to pee is one of the reasons that hamper their sleep at night.

o There's also a general discomfort. Women often find it difficult to find a comfortable sleeping position. Did you know that most women complain that they cannot find the right sleeping position? Yes, and what's more is that it can hamper their circulatory system in the later half of the pregnancy and cause swelling in the ankles, feet, and hands.

o Another reason for insomnia during the eighth month of pregnancy is heartburn. While women in the eighth month can experience heartburn all throughout the day, the sensation usually worsens at night. It's advisable that your partner eats smaller meals and avoids greasy foods.

o Women also face leg cramps at night which also leads to insomnia. This happens because of all the extra weight they're carrying throughout the day.

o Some women also complain of nasal congestion at night which makes it problematic for them to fall asleep. The membranes inside the nose swell, which is why they produce a greater amount of mucus than ever before. This leads to a perpetually stuffy nose, especially at night. You can advise your partner to use nasal sprays.

- **Wrist pain.** At around 33 weeks into the pregnancy, your partner will experience wrist pain. It comes as numbness or achiness in the wrist area or even the fingers. Just like the other tissues present in your body, the tissues in your wrist also retain excess fluid during pregnancy. This leads to an increase in pressure in the carpal tunnel region. This pain is also known as carpal tunnel syndrome. The intensity of the syndrome varies from person to person. For some people, it can be in the form of mild irritation, while for others, it can be a serious pain.

- **Increased libido.** At about 33 weeks of pregnancy, many women experience a sudden increase in libido. It's not unsafe to have sex during pregnancy. You might have to make some adjustments for sure but it's not impossible. Sex is fine until the labor starts or water breaks for your partner.

- **Numbness, tingling fingers.** This is also the result of carpal tunnel syndrome that I just explained above. The pain specifically occurs when the pressure falls on the median nerve in the wrist. The median nerve is responsible for several important functions, including the movement of the thumb and also supplying feelings to parts of the ring finger, middle finger, index finger, and thumb. So, when the median nerve is under pressure, these fingers can feel numb and have a tingling sensation.

- **Big baby bump.** Your partner might be finding it harder to tighten their seat belt nowadays because of the big baby bump. However, it's still important that they put on that seat belt irrespective of where they sit in the car. For some women, they might look more pregnant than they are, and this is completely normal too. This can be because they're either having multiple pregnancies or they have gained too much weight. Whichever it is, don't let your partner be too hard on themselves for it. Everybody is different, and there's no set formula as to what one should look like at a particular month.

- **Fatigue.** Fatigue during pregnancy is probably something that will start right in the first trimester and continue until you give birth. The degree to which each woman experiences fatigue often varies, but everyone experiences it to a certain degree. During the eighth month, which is the third trimester, your partner is carrying all that extra weight in the belly for so long that they're bound to feel tired. On top of this, they will also be dealing with problems like frequent urination and sleeping issues, which makes it harder to keep their energy levels high. Make sure your partner takes adequate rest whenever possible.

- **Dizziness.** When the uterus puts pressure on the blood vessels, your partner will feel dizzy. In the eighth month, the uterus has almost maxed out and is thus pressing on the blood vessels around it. This is why you'll notice when your partner lies down and then tries to get up; they feel dizzy. This is because when they lie down, the uterus blocks the blood flow from the heart to the extremities. Doctors often advise sleeping on their side to avoid this symptom. You must watch out for your partner falling due to dizziness. To avoid lightheadedness, you must ask them to stand up slowly and hold something while doing so.

- **Rash on the belly.** This is also termed the pruritic urticarial papules and plaques of pregnancy (PUPPP) rash, and it's an extremely frustrating and painful condition for pregnant women. It isn't harmful to the baby or the mother, but the rash itself can be irritating. These are mostly hive-like bumps that form on the belly around the area of the stretch marks, and then they can spread to other parts of the body as well. These rashes usually show up after week 35 of the pregnancy. The chances of a woman getting this rash increase if they're white and are carrying a male fetus, carrying twins or triplets, and this is their first pregnancy. About 1 in 160 pregnancies will face the PUPPP rash (Miles, 2021b). The itching from this rash is so irritating that it often makes it hard to concentrate on day-to-day activities for women.

- **Leaking urine.** Another common symptom around the eighth month is leaking urine. There's no need to worry about this as this is completely normal. We already spoke about how the uterus is increasing the pressure on the bladder, making your partner go to the bathroom an increased number of times. Apart from that, increased pressure on the bladder also leads to leaking urine. This is often referred to as stress incontinence because the leaking happens when your partner is doing some physical activity or when she laughs, sneezes, or coughs. About 41% of pregnancies suffer from stress incontinence (Sangsawang & Sangsawang, 2013).

Changes in the Baby

At 32 weeks, there are a lot of changes going on. About 97% of babies are born with their head first (Gardberg et al., 2011). As the due date comes closer, the babies start preparing for birth, and they tend to turn upside down at this stage. By the time a woman reaches 32 weeks, 85% of babies are already positioned in a head-down manner. So, now, without any further ado, let's take a look at the changes going on inside the womb.

- **The kicking baby.** By 32 weeks, the babies start to show the startle or Moro reflex. This is when a very loud noise or movement is made, it can surprise or startle the baby, and it will suddenly throw its legs and arms away from its body. After that, it will bring them back in. This reflex is present in the baby even when it's born but tends to go away after a few months.

- **Hair and nails grow.** By 32 weeks, the nails and hairs of the baby have also grown. The peach fuzz has come out, and babies are gearing up for their life outside the womb.

- **Soft flexible skull.** The bones of the baby are now fully developed, and they're a bit malleable and soft, especially the skull area. The plates of the skull will overlap one another so that the shape appears like that of a bullet and the baby easily passes out through the birth canal. It's often said that babies have a cone-head-like appearance; otherwise, it would be difficult to fit them through the narrow birth canal. In fact, did you know that one or two areas of the baby's skull will remain soft even after a year has passed after they're born? Yes, and these areas have a special term— fontanelles. They're normal gaps in the skull that are responsible for allowing the baby's brain to develop.

- **Smoothening of skin.** Your baby will be rapidly losing all the wrinkles on its skin around the 33-week mark. Their skin will become less transparent and red, and they will look less alien-like. The baby plumps up and becomes ready for life outside the womb.

- **Lots of movement.** The baby is running out of space inside the womb by now, and it's becoming quite snug inside. Hence, the baby might not be doing somersaults, but the level of kicking should still remain the same, even though the intensity of punches might become a little less.

- **Can see the color red.** By the 34th week, the baby starts seeing its first color, and it sees red all around. Hence, it's safe to say that it's during this week that the cone cells of the eyes develop, and the baby is able to see the inside of the uterus, which is red in color.

- **If your baby is born this week, it's fine.** Most women are worried about preterm labor, but you must know that if babies are born between 34 and 37 weeks, there's usually no problem, and they will be doing just fine. At 34 weeks, they look almost like a full-term baby even though they aren't fully mature. Having said that, it's true that they might encounter some health issues like difficulty breathing, difficulty feeding, and jaundice, but they will do well if proper care is given. At 34 weeks, the survival rate of preterm babies is very high, and the risk of disabilities that usually occur in the case of preterm babies is low.

- **Amniotic fluid recedes.** At 34 weeks, the amniotic fluid is at its peak. But at 35 weeks, it starts receding. By this time, the baby is floating in almost a quart of amniotic fluid. The fluid will now keep decreasing until your partner gives birth.

- **Physical development is mostly done.** By this time, the physical development of the baby is almost done. The kidneys have developed fully, and the liver has also gained the ability to process some of the waste products. The next few weeks are spent mostly by putting on more weight. However, you must keep in mind that the end of the pregnancy is the time when the baby's brain growth of the baby is still going on.

So, this section has given you a comprehensive idea of all the changes that go on in the baby during the eighth month of pregnancy. Between disturbed sleep cycles and headaches, your partner might find it difficult to get some much-needed rest, so let's take a look at some of the ways in which you can be of help.

How Can You Help?

At this point in the pregnancy, it's likely that you're taking time off from work and taking care of your part—splitting time between doing chores and preparing for the new member. In this section, we'll talk about some specific things you would want to start thinking about now.

Is This Your Second Pregnancy?

If this is your second pregnancy, check the condition of the baby gear from the older child. Is it safe to be reused? If it is, then there's nothing better than that. It will be good for your wallet too. Before you start shopping for baby gear, always check what things you already have at home that are already in good condition. One of the best things to reuse are clothes. Babies grow so fast that there's no point wasting so much money on buying more new clothes when you already have the ones from the older child. Similarly, you can also reuse shoes that have only been worn a couple of times. You can also preserve the crib of your older kid and then reuse it for your newborn.

Read Up on Baby Care

Once the baby is born, you won't have much time on your hands to read up about baby care. So, utilize all the time you have now. You need to maintain the good health of your baby in their earliest years because that's when most of the development happens. Remember, healthy babies grow up to become healthy adults. For proper baby care, you'll also have to take them to a doctor for routine checkups irrespective of whether they're sick or not. This will allow the doctor to evaluate the overall development of the child and check for any potential concerns. Reading up on baby care will help you gain such important knowledge prior to when you actually need to apply it in real life.

Pack a Hospital Bag

Next, comes the most important step of the eighth month. This is when you need to pack a hospital bag with your partner. If you're not sure where to start and the process seems overwhelming, don't worry; I've got your back. I've already done it before in my life, and from my experience, I'll give you some handy tips (you can thank me later!).

- **For labor.** If you're packing the bag for labor, here are some things that you should not forget:

    o Keep your antenatal notes on you wherever you go. You never know when they come in handy.

    o Pack some drinks and snacks. Trust me, labor can be long, so it's definitely not a bad idea to pack some food and drink for both you and your partner.

    o Labor rooms are usually warm, so you must pack some loose and comfortable clothing, for example, T-shirts or nightdresses—whatever your partner feels comfortable in.

o   Take water in a spray bottle along with a face towel or flannel. This will help your partner stay fresh and cool.

o   You can also take a game to play, or something to watch, listen to, or read—whatever your partner prefers because distractions have often been proven to be helpful in the early stages of labor.

o   It's important to keep your partner's hair out of the way; otherwise, they might feel irritated, hence, take a headband or hair bobbles.

o   If your partner feels uncomfortable with dry or chapped lips, take some lip balm.

o   A camera or your mobile phone must be ready.

o   Keep some change for the car park or taxi.

o   If you want to use a TENS machine, then carry one.

o   Toiletry items like toothpaste, toothbrush, facewash, shampoo, shower gel, or anything else that she wants should be packed.

o   Spare underwear for yourself is necessary.

o   Any chargers for your devices will be essential.

o   Have a change of clothes ready.

o   Any medications that you or your partner need are a must.

- **For after the birth.** If you're packing a bag for after the birth, here are some things that you must carry:

  o formula, teats, and sterile bottles if you've decided on bottle feeding

  o loose shirts or front-opening nightdresses that will make it easier to breastfeed or even snuggle the baby with skin-to-skin contact

  o 6–7 pairs of knickers (you might even want to bring disposable ones for your partner)

  o super absorbent maternity pads or sanitary pads for your partner

  o slippers

  o a light dressing gown

  o sanitary towels that are extra-absorbent (these will be helpful for after birth when there will be bleeding)

  o breast pads that will help in absorbing the leaking breast milk (if your partner isn't planning on breastfeeding then you'll need more of these)

  o a couple of nursing or ordinary bras (keep in mind the size of the bras because your partner's breasts will be a bit larger than usual)

  o nipple cream (this is especially important for women who are planning on breastfeeding so that the cream can heal the cracked or sore nipples which usually occur in the early breastfeeding days) o approximately five sleepsuits for the baby

o clothes for your partner to come home in (remember to pack loose clothes because she'll still have a bit of a bump)

o a shawl or a baby blanket

o cotton wool

o a pack of newborn nappies

o clothes for your baby to bring them home in

How is Your Partner Feeling?

Pregnancy is always a mix of feelings, and there's no guarantee that your partner is feeling happy all day long because of the approaching motherhood. There might be days she's feeling alone or worried. On those days, you have to be there for her by her side. Worry is a woman's common friend, especially in the case of an unplanned or first pregnancy. It's important that you don't neglect mental health during pregnancy. Mothers often don't get the help they need even when they're anxious or depressed. Their feelings often go unnoticed. Don't let that happen to your partner.

Ask for Help If You Feel Overwhelmed

We've been talking about your partner for way too long, but that doesn't mean you'll suppress your feelings even when you feel overwhelmed. Becoming a dad is definitely a rewarding experience, but along with that comes a lot of ups and downs too. If you want to support your partner through this pregnancy, you yourself first have to stay in a strong position mentally. So, if you're feeling overwhelmed, which is completely normal, ask for help. Make sure you talk to your partner about your worries. This will ensure that you both are on the same page regarding things. Having these conversations will also ensure less stress for both of you and will act as a constant source of reassurance.

You'll probably run into new challenges almost every day now that you're becoming a dad, but it's important that you learn to adapt to changes instead of having a fixed mindset. No one expects you to know everything all at once. You're trying to know things, and that's what matters. Reach out to doctors and family members who truly care for you. Most importantly, amidst all the chaos, don't forget to set aside some "me time" with your partner. This will strengthen your bond and help you both relax and decompress.

Get a TENS Machine

If you don't know it already, a transcutaneous electrical nerve stimulation (TENS) machine is a specialized device for pain relief. It utilizes a mild electrical current, and the machine is quite helpful when your partner is still in the early stages of labor. If you do decide to get a TENS machine for your partner to help with pain relief, then you need to get the ones that are particularly designed for use in maternity purposes.

Now, those who aren't acquainted with a TENS machine might be wondering how it works and whether it's harmful. Well, let me break it down for you. Small pads will be attached to your partner's skin, and small electrical pulses will be sent through them. The pulses will then reach your partner's tissues through the muscles. Your partner might feel a buzzing or tingling sensation, and it might be weaker or stronger, and it all depends on what level you've set the machine. Your partner will be able to hold the controller of the machine in their hands while they're in labor. They can even choose not to, and in that case, you can clip it to their clothing.

The electrical signs work by blocking the pain signals of your partner's body and don't allow them to reach the brain. Your partner also feels less anxious because, with the TENS machine, they feel as if they're in more control of the labor process. The pulses also stimulate the release of endorphins or feel-good hormones, which automatically make your partner feel better. Apart from all this, the pulses also act as a distraction from the contractions.

Get a Car Seat for Taking Your Baby Home

You'll need to install a proper car seat before you visit the hospital for labor and delivery. Car seats should be facing the rear of the car, and they have to be installed in the backseat. You should also try changing the length of the straps and also try locking and unlocking the buckle while you're still at the store to check everything is working properly. Every seat comes with a weight and height limit, so you need to check those before buying so that you know when exactly you need to change the seat while your newborn grows, and trust me, babies grow quite fast! If you're getting a used car seat instead of a new one, don't forget to ensure that it has not been in an accident and that it has not expired yet.

If you want to stay updated, then register your car seat with your specific manufacturer online, and you'll continue receiving all timely updates. Once the installation process is done, you need to take the car seat to the inspection station, where it will be checked for any discrepancies.

Get a Crib and a Baby Monitor

Since you're bringing your baby home, one of the essential things you need to buy before labor is a crib, and the eighth month is the perfect time to do so. A good chunk of the first few months of your baby will be spent in this crib and hence, you should be careful while buying it. If you're living in a small apartment, you might be drawn toward buying a mini crib, but let me tell you something: Your baby is going to quickly outgrow it, so keep this in mind before you settle for a mini crib.

Some other factors to keep in mind before buying a crib are as follows:

- The crib bars should have a specific width, and experts suggest that the gap should not be more than 2 $\frac{3}{8}$ in. (U.S. Consumer Product Safety Commission, n.d.). If it's more than that, it can be dangerous for the baby.

- Buy mattresses that don't sag under the weight of your baby. They should be firm and solid. Moreover, they should be the perfect size for your crib, reaching every corner.

- Headboards should not have any decorative cutouts and must be solid. This will ensure that the corners don't have things on which there's a risk for the baby's clothing to get stuck.

- If possible, go for an adjustable mattress. The ideal height for the crib's rail is 26 in from the top of the mattress (U.S. Consumer Product Safety Commission, n.d.).

- The crib should be sturdy, and it should not wobble in any way.

- Drop-side cribs aren't any safer as previously thought by parents.

- There shouldn't be any nails or screws sticking out of the crib that might hurt the baby.

- If you've bought a crib on wheels, the wheels must have a lock mechanism that is sturdy.

Now that you're aware of all the things you should look for in a crib, let's move on to the baby monitor, which is yet another essential thing you need to buy before your partner goes into labor. Some things that you should consider are as follows:

- The foremost factor that should be on your mind is the video quality. Never compromise on that.

- The sound quality also needs to be top-notch. Only then will you be able to hear all kinds of sounds in the room.

- Make sure the baby monitor has night vision. This ensures that you're able to keep an eye on the baby while you're sleeping in the other room.

Preterm Labor and Premature Birth

Women often fear preterm labor during the eighth month of pregnancy. Preterm labor occurs when regular contractions start happening in the region of the cervical opening between week 20 and week 37 of pregnancy. If premature labor starts, it could lead to premature birth. The risks for the baby are higher if premature labor starts earlier on in the pregnancy. Hence, it's essential for you as the partner to know everything related to premature labor and be prepared in case such a situation arises.

Symptoms

Let's discuss some of the signs of preterm labor. If your partner is undergoing preterm labor, the cervix will undergo a change. These changes include dilation, that is, opening of the cervix, and effacement, that is, thinning of the cervix. Some other signs include:

- pressure in the lower abdomen and pelvic regions

- a change in vaginal discharge (there might be more mucus, or it can be more watery or bloody)

- increase in the amount of vaginal discharge

- mild abdominal cramps along with diarrhea (sometimes without diarrhea)

- water breaks with a trickle or gush of fluid

- uterine tightening or regular or frequent contractions

- dull ache in the lower back

When Should You Rush to the Doctor?

If you notice signs of preterm labor in your partner, you should rush to the doctor's office immediately. If you call the doctor, they might ask you to stop what your partner is doing immediately and then lie on their left side for about an hour and see if the contractions go away. If they don't, then rush to the doctor's office immediately. Ask them to drink plenty of water (about two to three glasses) at once.

However, there's a simple rule to figure out whether you're truly in labor and whether it's time for you to go to the hospital. It's called the 5-1-1 rule. You need to keep a timer handy if you want to figure this out. Active labor is when your contractions are happening approximately five minutes apart from each other. They will last for about one minute each, and the same has been happening for about one hour. If this matches her description, it's time for you and your partner to grab the hospital bag and go to the hospital.

What Are the Risks Involved?

Preterm labor does not come with a warning and thus, it can happen to anyone. Some common problems that affect premature babies are:

- temporary pauses in breathing while the baby is asleep (apnea of prematurity)

- underdeveloped lungs (bronchopulmonary dysplasia)

- abnormal blood flow in the heart (patent ductus arteriosus [PDA])

- blood infection or neonatal sepsis

- inflammation of the intestines (necrotizing enterocolitis)

- bleeding in the brain (intraventricular hemorrhage)

- underdeveloped blood vessels in the eye (retinopathy of prematurity)

Complications and Preventions

There are some steps that you can take to avoid the complications of premature labor and birth, and they're as follows.

- **Seek regular prenatal care.** When your partner seeks regular prenatal care, it offers both of you vital information regarding the pregnancy and also the development of the fetus. It also gives you information about factors that could probably put the pregnancy at risk. Knowing about all this beforehand helps you stay aware and take the necessary precautionary measures to avoid anything unwanted.

- **Eat healthily.** Eating nutritious food during pregnancy is important for the development of the fetus in many ways. It aids in healthy birth weight and proper brain development and also decreases the chance of any birth defects. When your partner follows a balanced diet, they don't suffer from problems like anemia or other nutritional deficiencies which can further affect the baby.

- **Avoid risky substances.** Smoking has been found to increase women's chances of preterm labor. The more you expose yourself to smoking, the more your chances of having a premature birth. Some other risky substances that have the same effect include recreational drugs like methamphetamine, cocaine, and marijuana, and pain medications containing opioids. If your partner is a smoker and pregnant but looking for ways to quit, you can talk to her doctor because they can help provide support in this matter.

- **Spaced pregnancies.** It's advisable that you wait at least a period of 18 months from giving birth to getting pregnant again if you want to avoid preterm labor. Pregnancies are often associated with adverse birth outcomes when couples don't space out the pregnancies enough.

- **Be cautious with assisted reproductive technology (ART).** There have been several studies that reveal the fact that babies, when conceived through ART, have a higher chance of being born preterm (Bu et al., 2020).

- **Manage your chronic conditions.** If your partner has certain chronic conditions like high blood pressure or diabetes, then the chances of preterm birth increase. Hence, it's advisable that women manage these chronic conditions while there's still time if you want to prevent preterm labor.

From building the perfect nursery to announcing your baby's arrival (if you haven't done so yet), there's a lot on your plate this month, so I hope this chapter has been able to help you sort some things out. The next chapter looks at what you can expect in month 9 of the pregnancy.

Chapter 9:

Month 9—It's Time to Meet the Baby

Fatherhood is the greatest thing that could ever happen. You can't explain it until it happens—it's like telling someone what water feels like before they've ever swam in it. –Michael Bublé

Now that you've reached the ninth month of pregnancy, the journey is coming to an end. Your partner's water may break any time now. I understand that you're going through all types of emotions and even yearning to hold your baby in your arms. I've been through the same feeling. It's euphoric. However, you have to stay calm and patient because you still have to help your partner through labor. Meanwhile, let's take a look at all the changes that are going to happen this month.

Changes in the Mom

Most babies are positioned for delivery by now with their heads in the downward direction. At 36 weeks, the baby is almost the size of romaine lettuce. Let's go through the changes that your partner has to go through in this final month.

- **Decreased appetite.** Since the baby has taken up almost all the space available in the uterus and has almost no wiggle room left, your partner will face difficulty eating even a normal-sized meal at once. It's okay; you don't have to force them to eat. Instead, make them eat small-sized meals multiple times a day at regular intervals to ensure they're getting proper nutrition. At this point, this is the best strategy you have.

- **Breathing becomes easier.** During this time in the final month of pregnancy, the baby starts to drop down, and hence, breathing becomes easier for women as the pressure shifts more towards the pelvis rather than the diaphragm. This process is also known as lightening. If this is the first time your partner is getting pregnant, then this process will happen only a few weeks before labor. However, if your partner has given birth before then, this process usually starts just before labor.

- **Lower abdominal pressure.** As described above, the baby begins to move down. This automatically creates additional pressure in the lower abdomen area. A direct result of this is that women have found it uncomfortable to walk in the last few days. The pressure on the bladder also increases; hence, your partner might have to pee more frequently than ever before. In some cases, the baby is very low. In such women, the discomfort is maximum in the vaginal region, and they feel a lot of pressure. In fact, some women complain as if they're carrying a bowling ball.

- **Almost full term.** Your partner may be feeling impatient and tired and happy all at the same time, but you have to remember that they're approaching a full term now.

- **Vaginal discharge or spotting.** In the last couple of weeks before labor, there's usually an increase in the amount of vaginal discharge. If the discharge contains a tinge of blood in it, it's a sign that labor isn't far and might start in a couple of days. But you need to call your partner's doctor immediately if there's any heavy bleeding.

- **Nesting instincts.** Women get nesting instincts in the last few weeks of pregnancy. But do you know what this nesting instinct is? Well, this is the sudden burst of energy that women experience with the help of which they organize and clean the house to make it ready for the baby. This final frenzy is usually brought about by the excessive adrenaline running through your partner's body, but don't be surprised if these instincts don't hit your partner at all because that is common too. However, it's important that your partner stays sensible during this nesting stage and doesn't try to do things that won't suit her physically; for example, she shouldn't lift anything heavy. You must keep an eye on her regarding such things.

- **Swollen ankles.** In the last few weeks, some swelling is totally common, but at the same time, if you notice any excessive swelling in the ankles and feet of your partner that have occurred suddenly, you must not waste any time and call the doctor right away. Swelling around the ankles coupled with puffiness of the face and sudden gain in weight are all symptoms of preeclampsia, so you can never be too careful.

- **Trouble sleeping.** With your partner being in the ninth month, it will be harder than ever for them to fall asleep at night due to all the discomfort they're facing. It's advisable that they don't overwork themselves during the day. Ask them to take rest whenever they can and feel like it.

- **Ripening cervix.** When you go for your partner's prenatal checkup this month, the doctor will check the cervix and perform an internal exam. They will do this to see if the cervix has started ripening, that is, whether it has started dilating, effacing, and softening. However, even if the doctor does check the cervix, there's no 100% sure method of telling the exact day of when your baby is going to come.

- **Leaking fluid?** Do you think your partner's water might have broken? If you think so, then you need to call the doctor immediately. For every woman, the water breaks differently. For some, it comes out slowly with only a slow leak or a small gush, whereas for others, there's a big gush of fluid when it comes out. This is a very important thing, and so you should not be making this diagnosis yourself. Even if you suspect a small leak, you should call the doctor immediately instead of taking matters into your own hands. In patients whose water breaks but the contractions are delayed, they will be induced.

- **Still going to look pregnant after the baby is out.** Most women have what is commonly known as a baby belly after giving birth which is why they look pregnant even after. It's completely normal, but with the right exercises after your recovery, this can be managed. So, if your partner is worried about getting into shape, tell her not to sweat about it too much.

Changes in the Baby

When you started this journey, you had heard references to the "nine-month-long journey," but now you're officially in the ninth month. Let's take a look at all the changes going on inside the womb.

- **Already head down; if not, an external cephalic version is scheduled.** It's most likely that your baby is already in the head-down position by now. However, in some cases, doctors suggest the external cephalic version. Sounds alien? Wait, let me explain it to you. It's when external pressure is applied to the woman's abdomen with the aim of manipulating the position of the baby and making it shift to the head-down position because it wasn't able to do so on its own.

- **Shedding lanugo and vernix caseosa.** All this time, the baby was covered in lanugo, and now it's time that they start shedding all of it. It's also time for them to shed the vernix caseosa, which is a waxy substance that covers their whole body and protects the skin from the amniotic fluid in which the baby remained for such a long time. Once the items are shed, the baby will swallow both of them and any other item that is secreted. This results in a mixture called meconium which is black in color, and this is also what forms the contents of the baby's first bowel movements.

- **Starts to move fast.** In the ninth month, doctors might advise pregnant women to keep a daily fetal movement count, also known as DFMC. On average, a healthy baby should move about 50–60 times a day. Your partner will also notice that the movements have become quite faster. Just like newborns, during the ninth month, babies sleep for almost 20 hours in the womb, and it's only for the remaining 4 hours that they're active. For most pregnant women, the baby's movement increases when they lie down.

- **Fully formed nails.** Both the toenails and fingernails of your baby have developed completely by the ninth month. Keep a trimmer ready because once your baby is born, it will soon need a trim.

- **Eye color.** Most parents are wondering around this time what the eye color of their baby would be, I guess you're under the same dilemma too. If that's the case, let me tell you something. You won't be able to tell the eye color right away. However, if the baby is born with brown eyes, the chances are that the eyes will stay brown later too. But if the baby is born with dark blue or steel gray eyes, then the color might change to brown, hazel, or green by the time your baby is nine months old. This happens because the colored part of the eye, also known as the iris, gains pigment mostly after birth, but as a rule of thumb, they won't get any lighter or blue.

- **Firm grasp.** When you get to hold your baby for the first time, you'll be able to tell that your baby has a firm grasp—all babies do.

- **The kicking baby.** As I mentioned a while before, your partner needs to monitor your baby's movements this month closely. In case they seem to decrease drastically, you have to let the doctor know about it immediately. The baby should be kicking and remain active right until the day of delivery. It's a sign of a problem whenever there's a noticeable slowing down of activity of the baby.

- **Plumping up inside.** The baby continues to plump up even in the ninth month. Do you know why? This extra layer of fat will help the baby regulate its body temperature once it's born. It's highly likely that your baby has already grown to about 20 in. (Venuti et al., 2020). As a general rule of thumb, boys tend to weigh more than girls.

- **Size check.** Your baby is the size of a watermelon now, with a length of approximately 19.7–20 in. and weighing somewhat around 7.57 lb (Venuti et al., 2020).

How Can You Help?

Your partner probably has several questions for the doctor right now, and it's completely normal for them to do so. In the meantime, here are some pointers that you might want to learn now before the baby comes.

Learn How to Hold the Baby

You probably have already dreamt a thousand times of holding your baby in your arms. Now that it's almost time for the little one to arrive, did you give a thought as to how you're going to hold the baby? If not, then it's high time you start practicing. Depending on the circumstance, there are different ways to hold a baby. You're probably nervous about holding your newborn for the first time, and that happens to all parents. The most important thing to remember while holding your baby is that you need to support its head. This is because until and unless your baby is about four months old, it won't develop head control. Hence, it's up to you as the parent to hold the head so that it doesn't flip back or front or from side to side when you hold them up.

- **Picking up a baby.** Let's say you're picking the baby up from a crib. In that case, you have to be extra careful to support not only their neck and head but also their fontanelles. Slowly slide one hand under the neck to support the head and another hand at the bottom. Bend your knees a bit. Scoop them up only when you have a good grip on the baby. Slowly bring them close to your chest and then straighten your legs.

- **Lying position hold.** Now, let's see how you're going to hold the baby when it's in the lying position. Rest its head on your chest, and with your hand, cradle its head. Use the other arm to support the neck. In the crook of your elbow, place its head for extra support. With the other hand, support the bottom of your baby. This is a great position to talk to your baby, make eye contact with them, and build a bond in the initial days.

- **Upright position hold.** When you want to hold the baby in the upright position, you need to use one hand to support the neck and the head while they rest on your shoulder or chest. Use the other hand to support your baby's bottom.

How to Swaddle a Baby

Once your baby is born, you need to master the art of swaddling, so why not start preparing now? Swaddling is the process of wrapping your newborn in a piece of cloth, and it's quite an ancient method. This method will help your baby sleep soundly and stay calm. Do you know why? Well, the swaddle makes the baby feel as if it's still inside the womb, and so it feels safe. Swaddling also prevents the baby from going into a startle reflex since it cannot spread its arms and legs. It also keeps the baby warm and comfy until its own temperature control kicks into action.

Now, let's take a look at how you can swaddle a baby in a step-by-step manner.

- **Look for a flat surface.** You first need a flat surface where you can spread the swaddle blanket. It should be arranged in the shape of a diamond. The top corner needs to be folded down around 6 in.

- **Place your baby.** Bring your baby and place them face-up on the blanket. The position should be such that their head is just above the folded edge of the blanket.

- **Straighten the left arm.** Once you straighten your baby's left arm, you need to take the left side of the blanket and then wrap the blanket over the chest and left arm. Tuck the blanket nicely behind the right arm. If you've done it correctly, then the right arm should be free while the left arm should be covered.

- **Bring the bottom up.** Take the bottom corner of the blanket and fold it up over the baby's body. You have to tuck the corner under the chin beneath the first fold. Now straighten the right arm and do the same thing with the right side of the blanket as you did with the left side.

- **Secure the blanket.** Take the bottom of the blanket, twist it loosely, and tuck it nicely and safely underneath your baby.

Something that you need to keep in mind while swaddling the baby is that if you're doing it right, then the swaddle should not be too tight but snug. In order to check it, place two-three fingers between the baby and the blanket. The blanket should also be a little loose around the hip area.

Your Role in the Labor Room

If this is your first trip to the labor room and you're still wondering what your role is, then know this—your first and foremost duty is to support your partner. The worst thing about labor is that no one knows when it will start, and it can sometimes even end up in an emergency situation. I can understand that even if you're under a lot of stress, you have to stay strong for your partner.

- **Can you be in the labor room?** These days, it's becoming common for dads to choose to be inside the labor room during birth. However, it also depends on the hospital policies where you've chosen to deliver the child and your wife's decision. Some hospitals have restrictions while others actively encourage the dad's involvement, so you must ask about these things from before so that nothing comes as a surprise later on. Some hospitals restrict the entry of partners in the delivery room in case of cesarean births, so you need to ask about that too.

- **How can you prepare for the baby's birth?** Preparation is essential if you're indeed going to be inside the labor room and that is allowed by the hospital you've chosen. Preparing doesn't mean it will stop the unexpected from happening or that you can simply breeze through the labor and delivery process, but what it means is that you'll stay more aware. Being aware will ensure that you're able to help and support your partner in the way she needs you to. You can join antenatal classes that specifically prepare partners for the labor room.

- **How does your presence help?** Your presence helps in a lot of ways—more than you can imagine. You're your partner's emotional support system. You being there means a lot for them, especially during a time when they're in so much pain. Being in the labor room also means you're sharing the whole birth experience with your partner. Instead of waiting for an announcement from the doctor, when you're inside the labor room, you'll feel a part of the process.

- **What are the difficulties with being in the labor room?** Experts often say that some men feel helpless when they're in the delivery room simply because they cannot do anything to lessen the pain of their partner, but they have to simply stand there and watch her in pain. Hence, it's safe to say that a labor room experience is definitely not for the faint-hearted. Some dads even say that they have to follow the doctor's orders and hence, sometimes, when they're asked to step away, it feels like they're no longer needed in the labor room, and their presence doesn't matter. Some men also feel embarrassed about the labor procedures and gynecological examinations that are being performed in front of them.

- **Do you not want to be there?** It's completely okay if you feel that way. You first need to acknowledge to yourself that your feelings aren't out of the ordinary. There are several partners who don't feel comfortable being in the labor room due to various factors (some of them have even been mentioned above). If you feel that your partner or family members are expecting too much from you, you should have open communication with them instead of bottling up your feelings. If you feel that you might pass out seeing all that pain or that you might not be able to put up with so much blood or get queasy, don't ignore your fears because they're all legit. It's responsible of you to think of these things prior to labor so that no problem arises later on. Let your partner know that even if you're not inside the labor room, you'll always be waiting for them right outside if they need anything. Just try not to be so hard on yourself.

Prepare Them for Breastfeeding

Breastfeeding might be a woman's task, but there are so many things that you can do as a partner to support your wife during the process. Let's take a look at some of them.

Before the baby arrives:

- This is the right time for you to learn about the basics of breastfeeding.

- Talk to your partner and set up some breastfeeding goals because this will ensure that you both are on the same page.

- Join a breastfeeding class because this is going to be enlightening for soon-to-be-dads.

- When you take the tour of the birthing center or the hospital that you've chosen, ask about the breastfeeding practices followed there.

At the hospital:

- If you have a breastfeeding plan, share it with the hospital staff.

- Between each feeding, hold the baby in your arms and experience some skin-to-skin contact.

- If you see that your partner is struggling with breastfeeding (which is perfectly normal), ask for help from the hospital staff.

At home:

- Always remember that your partner has just given birth to the baby, and she's still recovering. When she's done breastfeeding the baby, you can bathe, soothe, cuddle, dress, change, and burp the baby. Don't leave your partner alone when she's breastfeeding. Keep her company and make sure she has enough to eat and drink too.

- Understand your baby's hunger cues so that you can immediately bring them to your partner for another round of breastfeeding.

- You need to go the extra mile to help your partner during the first few months. Help her with chores, do the laundry, clean the house, and cook whenever you can. If your partner says that she needs something while breastfeeding, bring it for her. If you have multiple children in the house, take care of them while your partner breastfeeds the newborn.

- New moms are usually tired and don't want too many visitors. So, it's your duty to limit the number of visitors as much as you can.

- Encourage your partner and make them feel good about themselves. Tell from how proud you're of them for delivering your child. Do something for her from time to time to make her feel special. She deserves that.

- There will be many people around you with passive negative comments about you and your partner's choice to breastfeed. You need to learn to defend your choice and not pay heed to what others think or say.

Buy Her Nursing Bras

In the initial months after pregnancy, when your partner is breastfeeding, normal bras aren't the right pair of lingerie. You need to buy your partner nursing bras. These bras are the right mix of comfort and support. These bras also have hooks and clasps in the front so that your partner can easily open them during breastfeeding. On top of that, the fabrics used in these bras are so comfortable and stretchable that it allows the breasts to breathe and leaves enough room for the fluctuating size of the breasts, especially before and after breastfeeding. These bras are also easily adjustable. These aren't underwired. If you buy underwired bras at this point, they will dig into the soft tissue of your partner, which isn't good for their health. Rest assured that with the nursing bras, the blood will flow freely and no damage will occur to the breast tissues.

Your Baby Is Ready to Meet the World

The day has finally arrived when your baby will meet the world, and you'll finally hold them in your arms. Let's quickly take a look at the series of events that will happen.

- **Water breaks.** Labor is definitely a unique experience for everyone. No two women will give you the same description of labor. Labor starts with the breaking of water. As explained before, for some women, the water might break with a gush, while for others, it might break with a trickle.

- **Planned delivery at home.** Here, you've decided before that your partner will be giving birth at home instead of going to the birthing center. But you also need to keep in mind that in case of this birth, you'll need to have someone highly experienced and qualified by your partner's side. This can be a certified professional midwife, a certified nurse midwife, a naturopathic or medical doctor specialized in obstetrics, or a midwife meeting international standards.

- **Unplanned delivery at home.** This can indeed be a scary experience when your partner has to give birth to your baby in case of an emergency when you had originally planned to give birth in a hospital or a birthing center. You've probably seen it a lot in TV medical dramas; however, in real life, it's not as common as you think it is. You first need to call 911 and tell them that you need a medical squad since your baby is coming. Keep your door unlocked so that the medical crew can get in immediately as they arrive. Grab blankets, sheets, and towels, and put one underneath your partner. Always deliver while sitting propped up or while lying down. Ask your partner to resist the urge to push and stay calm. Be gentle and guide the baby out as much as you can.

- **Get to the hospital.** If it's not an emergency and your partner's water has broken, get to the hospital or birthing center that you had chosen. Complete the admission process, and the doctors will guide you on the rest of the process.

- **Call the doctor or midwife.** On the way to the hospital, call your partner's doctor or midwife and let them know that the water has broken and that you're heading to the hospital.

- **Let the doctors do their thing.** Once you're in the hospital, you have to follow the doctor's orders. Don't try to deviate from their instructions. They're the experts, and they obviously know better, so the wiser thing would be to let the doctors do their thing.

- **The baby is here!** Labor can take a few minutes to even hours. Nobody knows how long it will take. But after the arduous process, your baby is finally here. Your little bundle of joy! If the delivery was uncomplicated, then the doctors usually give your partner a few minutes with the baby before they cut off the umbilical cord.

- **Postpartum functions.** After your partner delivers the baby, in about 30 minutes, she'll deliver the placenta, after which the uterus will go back to its original size. Postpartum care often involves managing sore breasts, leaking milk, vaginal tears, and urination problems.

- **Newborn tests.** After birth, your newborn will have to undergo certain tests which will evaluate their overall health and well-being. These will measure some vital signs and also the responsiveness of the baby. The five major factors that are checked during this time are heart rate, activity, color, breathing, grimace reflex response, and muscle tone.

- **If there's a problem.** In each of the above categories mentioned above, your baby will be given a score of 0–2, and then all five scores will be combined to get the overall Apgar score. The same evaluation will then again be done at one minute and then at five minutes. This test is very easy and quick and is mainly aimed at determining whether the baby can breathe on its own or needs some extra help. A normal score ranges between 7–10. If your baby's score also falls within this range, you can rest assured that no extra actions will be required. However, if the score is lower, it means your baby will need some extra help. Oxygen might have to be provided externally.

- **Feeding.** If your partner has decided on breastfeeding then she can start that as soon as the baby is given to her. For a first-time mom, the milk will probably not fully come for a day or two. But babies can get their nutrients from colostrum as well, which is the precursor to the actual breast milk. For some women, colostrum is yellowish and thick, whereas, for others, it's watery and thin. When the child starts sucking on your partner's breast, it will signal to the body that it's time to make the milk.

- **Sharing the news.** It's better to keep the first day simple. You can share the news with your closest family members and friends, and then you can ask them to pass the news along to others. Allow only your closest loved ones to meet the baby on the first day; otherwise, it can become overwhelming. It's best to avoid a parade of visitors.

Now that your baby is born, you're about to begin an entirely new phase in your life with your partner. Relax and enjoy the first day with your partner and your baby. The next chapter talks about how to take care of your baby and the mother after birth.

Chapter 10:

Month 10—After the Delivery

It's all about you not trying to decide what your daughter or son should be or what you want them to be, it's all about loving them no matter who they are or what they decide to do. –Magic Johnson

There are several emotions that you'll face as a new parent, but guilt is probably one that your partner will face the most. You might be wondering why. Well, we live in a society of high expectations. Everyone is on Facebook, where they see the so-called perfect lives of others and constantly compare themselves with what they see on the internet. It's very easy for new mothers to become traumatized and concerned about the smallest of things that you think are of no concern. One of the most common things that women feel guilty about is when they don't instantly feel motherly love. Most women are able to bond with their babies almost instantly, but there are also others who cannot and are more traumatized by the changes to their bodies. If your partner is going through the same phase, you have to be by their side instead of criticizing them for what they're feeling.

Another common guilt that women face is taking out time for themselves—they feel as if they have done something immensely wrong by trying to have some "me" time amidst all the chaos. You have to remind your partner that everyone deserves an outlet to recharge themselves and, in a way, reenergize because only then can they become good parents. It's time you tell your partner to drop their guilt because there's no use holding on to it for so long. It's normal to feel guilty, but at the same time, it's also perfectly normal to be overjoyed by having a small bundle of cuteness in your arms and feeling extremely emotional.

Taking Care of the Mother

Once you've become a parent, it will be the most beautiful phase of your life, and that too is an understatement. But at times, your partner might feel emotionally spent, and you have to step up to take care of her. In this section, we'll take a look at the various ways in which you can take care of your partner.

Create a New Normal

Bouncing back to normal life after pregnancy might sound easy, but in real life, it's really not such a cakewalk. Your partner's body has gone through a lot of changes, and sometimes it can take a toll on the woman's mental health too. As she tries to adjust to this new life after the baby, it's important that you remind her that her emotions and mind are also changing and so she needs to take some time out for herself and give herself the support she needs.

On some level, every couple waits for the pregnancy to end because that also means an end to the hectic days your partner and even you had been enduring for months! You were eagerly waiting for your days to return back to your usual routine. And now that you have your baby in your arms, this is probably the first time in your life that you're understanding what it really means for your life to be changed forever. What is important now for both you and your partner is to go with the flow. Eventually, your partner will find a rhythm that works for her and fall into it. After that, she can figure out a routine that works for her. Don't expect all this to happen overnight—it will definitely take a lot of time and patience.

Get Used to Lack of Sleep

Lack of sleep is a common problem that all mothers face after having a baby which results in them being tired almost all the time. But this phase where the baby is waking up multiple times a night is only for a couple of months—it won't last forever. Something that you can do to help your partner through this phase is to take turns keeping an eye on the crib through the night. If your baby is sleeping in your room, the trip to the crib will be shorter. Your partner might be up for the 3 a.m. breastfeeding sessions and might not need you during those hours, but you still need to show up. You can help with the diaper change while she rests. Moreover, cuddles during those hours count for some quality bonding time for the family. You shouldn't be missing them at all costs.

There might be times when you're feeling tired but remember, your partner is even more tired so take care of the baby during the day whenever you can and let your partner rest. Sure, you both need sleep, but you cannot forget the fact that your partner is also recovering physically after childbirth.

Keep an Eye on Her Mood

Did you know that 80% of new moms are affected by baby blues? (Baby Blues, 2019) Yes, but it's within a couple of weeks that these feelings will fade away. Baby blues are when a woman faces feelings of anxiety, restlessness, and crying due to the several hormonal changes that she has to go through. Once the hormone levels return back to normal, the baby blues fade out. It's completely normal not to be happy all the time, even as a new mother. But if you notice that your partner's symptoms aren't going away on their own even after weeks and she's facing severe irritability, sleep disruptions, and bouts of crying, you should consult a physician right away because it might be a case of postpartum depression. We'll talk about this subject in detail in the latter part of this chapter.

Be Good to Yourself

You both had to go through a lot of planning and drama, and after all that buildup to the climax, your baby is finally here. It's definitely a joyful moment, but the stress from the past nine months is going to take a toll on your health with a huge sense of responsibility slowly setting in. In fact, it has been found that 25% of new dads undergo paternal postnatal depression (PPND), and it's not even talked about as much as it should be (Kim & Swain, 2007).

You must know that it's common to feel overwhelmed and left out. After all, at the end of the day, even you are a human being and have feelings too. You need to take a rest in a timely manner and eat nutritious food to maintain good health.

If you think you have symptoms of PPND, then don't waste any time and consult an expert. If you feel that you don't want to go to an expert right away, talk to a friend or family member first, and take their advice if you want to but going to an expert is always the right course of action. Never hesitate to seek professional treatment when deep in your heart, you know that you need it.

Be Good to Her

As mentioned before, your partner is currently recovering from all the physical effects of childbirth. It's best if you take over some of the household chores for now. This will give your partner the opportunity to rest whenever she feels like it. If you can afford it, then get paid domestic help for a few days because it will give both of you the opportunity to get the rest you need and also give all your energy, attention, and focus to the baby.

It's natural for guests and relatives to come over to meet the newest member of the family, but it's your duty to ensure that these guests don't overstay their welcome because this will only be more overwhelming for both of you.

Small gestures go a long way in making sure you care for her. So, bring her something to eat when she's breastfeeding or give her a massage when you're free. Just go and give her a warm hug, and you'll see her face instantly light up with a smile.

Divide and Conquer

Unlike what society tells you, parenting is always a two-person job and ensures you're following the rules. Whether it's about changing the diaper or bathing the baby, divide the work, and it will become so much easier for both of you. Most dads have this feeling in the beginning that they're not cut out for this kind of job, but there's nothing to be so worried about! No one is born knowing how to swaddle a baby. There are some things that everybody has to learn and so will you. Take it one diaper at a time.

It's okay if you do things differently than your partner. You both are two different human beings, so it's only just that you'll be doing it differently, but at the end of the day, both of you love the baby, and that's what counts.

Be Patient When It Comes to Sex

Right now, after months of not being able to have sex properly, it might be the only thing on your mind, but you need to learn to be patient. Your partner is still recovering from childbirth, so you obviously can't have sex until and unless you get a green light from your partner's doctor first. The usual timeframe is usually four to six weeks after delivery. Moreover, when you do decide to move forward with it, make sure you're gentle with her. Take it slowly. You need to ask her what hurts and what feels good and what you can do to make it better. Remember, lubricant is going to be your best friend in the postpartum phase, so make the best use of that and focus on the foreplay.

Talk It Out

It's very common to suffer from self-doubt as a new parent, and your partner might be going through that phase right now as you're reading this book. It's nothing to worry about because every new parent has to undergo this at least once. You need to open up to your spouse about your own feelings, or your own self-doubts regarding baby care, and only then can you offer support to her feelings. Fear of flunking at the job can be nagging, and you're not the first person on this earth to experience this. When you both share each other's thoughts, you'll feel much lighter and better.

Taking Care of the Baby

You probably have some expectations about the first few weeks when your baby is born, but it's almost always harder than expected for new parents. From tough latch-on to sore nipples, your partner is already going through a lot, so let's take a look at some tips that will help you to help her take care of the baby.

Nursing

Most partners think that breastfeeding is a woman's job, but it can be done as a team if you're willing to help her out. Here are some practical ways to help out with the baby even if you're not physically breastfeeding them:

- Hold the baby or carry them in a sling. Settling the baby becomes easier with skin-to-skin contact.

- Massage your baby or bathe your baby to soothe them.

- Sometimes babies can be fussy. So, you can help by settling the baby down so that it becomes easier for your breastfeeding partner.

- After the breastfeeding session, take the baby for a diaper change or a burp.

Soothing

It's not always the duty of the mother to soothe the baby. Read these tips to know how you can soothe your child when your partner is busy with other chores or resting.

- The first step is to understand what your baby needs or the reason behind their crying. It might sound obvious now, but when your baby is crying for a long time, it can be hard to think straight and find a solution. The most common reason for crying in the case of a newborn is a dirty diaper because it irritates their skin.

- Rock and swing the baby because they love movement. Make repetitive and slow sounds as you rock them. This will surely soothe them in a few minutes.

- Try to do something silly. It often works with newborns. Maybe pretend to be a clown or make funny faces.

- Try wearing your baby in a sling. The warmth that radiates from your baby often calms them down.

Getting Partners Involved

The postpartum phase can be really rocky for some mothers, and it's essential that you stay by their side at all times. Some things that you can do for them during this period are:

- Your partner is mostly sleep-deprived. You should try your best to allow them to sleep. For this, you might have to work a bit harder to look after the baby, do household chores, and so on so that your partner can take a rest.

- When your partner is breastfeeding the baby, stay with them and make sure they have everything they need.

- It's important that you make your partner feel that she's never alone in this postpartum period. So, when she's nursing the child or breastfeeding it, sit with her and give her company.

- Most women feel guilty about asking for any help but you must understand that your partner's body has already gone through a lot and so, you must do whatever you can to help her with household chores.

- Make your partner feel special from time to time. Plan that date night, go for a movie date together, and set up a surprise for her—do all those things that will brighten up her day.

Going Out and About With the Baby

When you've had a newborn, don't hole up in the house. Try to go out whenever you can. Here are some tips that will make going out easier:

- Always stock your car with baby essentials before you go somewhere. Have some backup clothes for the baby, wipes, towels, diapers, paper towels, and an extra pair of shoes. When you keep these items in the car all the time, it will reduce your time to pack things when you're going on a trip.

- Always feed your baby before you leave for a place. Whether you're bottle feeding or breastfeeding, feeding the baby on the go will be a lot more stressful; hence feeding the baby just before it's time for you to go somewhere is one of the best ways to ensure your baby isn't hungry right after you leave home.

- Last but not least, don't stress too much. Parenthood is about adjusting to a lot of things. Having people around you who understand you completely is essential during this time.

Postpartum Depression

Now that you have had an idea about almost everything related to the baby and the mother in the postpartum period, let's talk about another important topic that's mainly linked to the psychological, social, and chemical changes that happen in the mother's body after she has a baby, that is, postpartum depression.

Causes

There isn't enough research to determine the exact cause of postpartum depression but based on what is available so far, it happens because of a sudden drop in hormones in the female body. During pregnancy, the progesterone and estrogen levels increase almost 10 times than what they usually are but right after the delivery, there's a sharp decrease in the amount of these hormones. In addition to this, the woman also has to go through several psychological changes after delivery which add to this problem.

Symptoms

Some of the symptoms of postpartum depression are as follows:

- feeling guilty, hopeless, worthless, and sad

- not feeling like eating anything or changes in appetite

- feeling on edge most of the time

- crying excessively for no reason at all

- loss of interest in things that your partner enjoyed before

- thoughts of committing suicide

- trouble sleeping and loss of energy

- thoughts of harming the baby

- feeling anxious

- difficulty focusing

Treatment

Depending on how seriously your partner has been affected by postpartum depression, the recovery time may vary. Your partner's doctor will be suggesting a mental health professional for this problem. Some common treatment options include psychotherapy, antidepressant medicines, anti-anxiety medicines, and even participation in various support groups. If your partner isn't at all stable, then the doctor might advise you to take her to a treatment center until things come under control. Some women assume that just because they're breastfeeding, they won't be able to take medicines for depression, but that's just a myth. Talk to your partner's doctor today.

The baby is here now. Many sleepless nights and tiring schedules await you—but also a lifetime of having a family, laughter, and love.

Conclusion

When you find out that you're pregnant, that is probably the best day in the life of both you and your partner. But as new moms and dads-to-be, no one is really prepared for the trials of the nine months that lie ahead. The aim of this book was to help you become better prepared as a partner so that you can understand the female body and be there for her whenever she needs you. However, taking care of your partner and also keeping the romance alive are two tasks that you'll have to do hand-in-hand and even though it might seem easy now, it won't be so easy when the time comes.

Becoming a parent is filled with love and hope, and you have to remember that you're on this journey together. There might be a mix of emotions coming your way, but there's nothing that you can't deal with when you're together.

Your partner will be anxious throughout the pregnancy. You need to find ways to soothe, calm, and reassure her whenever she's afraid of something. Did you know that research shows women have a better pregnancy experience when their partners are actively involved in the process? (Rhodes et al., 2021) Yes, and it will be a great relief for them too because they'll know they have someone to rely on.

For first-timers, childbirth can be overwhelming. So, talk with your partner about everything that goes on in her mind. Whether it's anxiety about the type of mom she'll be or fear regarding the upcoming procedures, talk to her and share your thoughts. You shouldn't hold back from sharing your fears too because, at the end of the day, you're a team. If you're holding back, your partner will know, and she won't open up to you.

Go the extra mile to help her around the house. Sweep the floors or maybe whip up a double batch of chili so that you can reheat it and serve it whenever you want to. This will reduce the workload to a great extent. Give her a foot massage or a gentle hug randomly throughout the day. It's definitely going to make her smile.

When the pregnancy nears completion, help your partner pack the hospital bag. Fill it with some snacks, toothpaste, a toothbrush, a change of clothes, magazines, books to read, and all the other things that we've already discussed inside the book. Don't wait until the umpteenth minute to pack this bag. It will only result in more chaos. Have it ready before time because this will also prove to be useful in case of an early delivery where you need to rush through the door immediately. While you pack the bag, make sure to put some fancy things in without her noticing, like some cute face towels or some chocolate. This will definitely make her happy when she's in the labor room or after delivery.

Get involved in all the medical stuff. This means going on prenatal visits with her. However, before that, you must also ask your partner how involved she wants you to be and whether she feels comfortable with you on these medical visits. If she's okay with you coming along, make it a point not to miss any of the important days because there will be milestone appointments for the ultrasound where you'll hear the first heartbeat or get to know the gender of the baby.

That being said, life won't be easier for your partner as the due date comes closer. She will face sleeping issues and also face a surge of emotions. Make it easier for her to spend the days. Get her a body pillow. Cuddle with her before sleeping or maybe turn on the AC/fan if she's too hot.

Last but not least, you'll have a lot on your plate throughout these nine months. With all the texting, shopping, and daily chores, sometimes it's easy to get lost between your responsibilities and forget a few important tasks in between, which is why it's important for partners to have a wingman. If you haven't chosen yours already, it's high time you choose someone now.

A happy pregnancy isn't hard to achieve when you have your partner with you. An educated and aware partner is worth even more. If this book has helped you learn more about the changes going on with your partner's body and how you can be a better support system, leave a review.

About the Author

Rocky Hunter is a father of two and a highly recommended certified parenting coach. He leads parenting classes, teaching a wide array of conscious parenting techniques right from the beginning to dads and moms who think they're doing everything wrong.

As a parenting coach, Rocky has come across many new dads who aren't as aware of the process of pregnancy and are mighty confused about their roles in the entire journey. He has also come across many women who find pregnancy an easier experience with the support of an educated partner. Countless researchers attest to this fact too. Rocky believes in active parenting from dads, and it all starts as soon as you both first know you'll be parents.

References

A-Z Quotes. (n.d.). *John Green quotes.* https://www.azquotes.com/quote/548404

American Pregnancy Association. (2019, January 25). *Baby Blues.* https://americanpregnancy.org/healthy-pregnancy/first-year-of-life/baby-blues/

Batcha, B. & Srinivasan, H. (2021, September 14). *Here's a nine-month plan to get your finances in check before baby arrives.* Parents. https://www.parents.com/pregnancy/considering-baby/financing-family/a-nine-month-plan-for-getting-your-familys-finances-in-order-pre-baby/

de Bellefonds, C. (2022, June 24). *Pregnancy hunger: How to handle increased appetite in pregnancy.* BabyCenter. https://www.babycenter.com/pregnancy/health-and-safety/im-pregnant-and-constantly-hungry-how-can-i-manage-my-weight_10394933

de Bellefonds, C. (2022, August 15). *7 signs you're ovulating.* What to Expect. https://www.whattoexpect.com/getting-pregnant/fertility/five-ways-to-tell-you-are-ovulating.aspx

Bologna, C. (2017, January 31). *Justin Timberlake's best quotes on the "humbling" experience of parenthood.* HuffPost. https://www.huffpost.com/entry/justin-timberlakes-best-quotes-on-the-humbling-experience-of-parenthood_n_5890ae39e4b0c90eff001c4f

Bologna, C. (2019, August 11). *14 sweet parenting quotes from Chris Hemsworth.* HuffPost. https://www.huffpost.com/entry/chris-hemsworth-parenting-quotes_l_5d4b1d2ee4b09e7297404c8c

Brar, D. (2020, April 2). *How positive self-talk can help you.* BabyCenter. https://www.babycenter.com/family/motherhood/how-positive-self-talk-can-help-you_40007084

Bright Horizons. (2021, July 15). *Pregnancy for dads: A father's role before the baby arrives.* https://www.brighthorizons.com/family-resources/pregnancy-for-dads-a-fathers-role-before-the-baby-arrives

Bu, Z., Zhang, J., Hu, L. & Sun, Y. (2020). Preterm birth in assisted reproductive technology: An analysis of more than 20,000 singleton newborns. *Frontiers in Endocrinology, 11.* https://doi.org/10.3389/fendo.2020.558819

Bullivant, S. B., Sellergren, S. A., Stern, K., Spencer, N. A., Jacob, S., Mennella, J. A. & McClintock, M. K. (2004). Women's sexual experience during the menstrual cycle: Identification of the sexual phase by noninvasive measurement of luteinizing hormone. *Journal of Sex Research, 41*(1), 82–93. https://doi.org/10.1080/00224490409552216

Calton-Weekes, J. (2018). *Why you're experiencing bleeding gums in pregnancy and how to treat it.* Mother & Baby. https://www.motherandbaby.co.uk/pregnancy/health-and-wellness/why-you-might-get-bleeding-gums-in-pregnancy-and-how-to-treat/

Cleveland Clinic. (2020, April 16). *Stages of pregnancy & fetal development.*

https://my.clevelandclinic.org/health/articles/7247-fetal-development-stages-of-growth

Dailey, K. (2021, March 19). *How to create a birth plan.* WebMD. https://www.webmd.com/baby/guide/how-to-create-a-birth-plan

Darwin, Z., Domoney, J., Iles, J., Bristow, F., Siew, J. & Sethna, V. (2021). Assessing the mental health of fathers, other co-parents, and partners in the perinatal period: Mixed methods evidence synthesis. *Frontiers in Psychiatry, 11.* https://doi.org/10.3389/fpsyt.2020.585479

Dasher, E. (2021, August 20). *Magnesium during pregnancy.* BabyCenter. https://www.babycenter.com/pregnancy/diet-and-fitness/magnesium-in-your-pregnancy-diet_659

Dunkin, M. A. (2010, January 14). *Back pain in pregnancy.* WebMD. https://www.webmd.com/baby/guide/back-pain-in-pregnancy

Eco, U. & Weaver, W. (2007). *Foucault's pendulum.* Harcourt.

Fatherly. (2021, February 10). *What all dads need to recognize about modern fatherhood.* https://www.fatherly.com/parenting/welcome-to-fatherhood

Frothingham, S. (2020). *Can a baby be too active in the womb?* Healthline. https://www.healthline.com/health/pregnancy/active-babies

Gardberg, M., Leonova, Y. & Laakkonen, E. (2011). Malpresentations - Impact on mode of delivery. *Acta Obstetricia et Gynecologica Scandinavica, 90*(5), 540–542. https://doi.org/10.1111/j.1600-0412.2011.01105.x

Gates, M. (2021, August 4). *When does morning sickness start, peak, and end?* BabyCenter. https://www.babycenter.com/pregnancy/your-body/when-does-morning-sickness-start-peak-and-end_40005756

Gates, M. (2022, March 21). *11 weeks pregnant.* BabyCenter. https://www.babycenter.com/pregnancy/week-by-week/11-weeks-pregnant

Gavrilovic, M. (2008, June 15). *Obama's Father's Day message.* CBS News. https://www.cbsnews.com/news/obamas-fathers-day-message/

Getz, M. (2022, July 14). *Fetal development: Your baby's sense of taste.* BabyCenter. https://www.babycenter.com/pregnancy/your-baby/fetal-development-your-baby-s-sense-of-taste_20005028

Hattori, K. (2014, April 1). *What makes a compassionate man?* Greater Good. https://greatergood.berkeley.edu/article/item/what_makes_a_compassionate_man

Horowitz, J. M., Parker, K., Graf, N. & Livingston, G. (2017, March 23). *How paid leave impacts gender and caregiving.* Pew Research Center. https://www.pewresearch.org/social-trends/2017/03/23/gender-and-caregiving/

Johnson, T. C. (2002, May 27). *Gain weight safely during your pregnancy.* WebMD. https://www.webmd.com/baby/guide/healthy-weight-gain

Kelly, A. L. (2018, December 18). *Accentuating the positive when you're pregnant.* Parents. https://www.parents.com/pregnancy/mylife/emotions/accentuating-the-positive-when-youre-pregnant/

Kim, P., & Swain, J. E. (2007). Sad dads: Paternal postpartum depression. *Psychiatry (Edgmont (Pa. : Township), 4*(2), 35–47. https://www.ncbi.nlm.nih.gov/pmc/articles/PMC2922346/

Lewsley, J. (2021, December). *Tried and tested ways to soothe a crying baby for partners.* BabyCenter. https://www.babycentre.co.uk/a1005167/tried-and-tested-ways-to-soothe-a-crying-baby-for-partners

Livingston, G. & Parker, K. (2019, June 12). *8 facts about American dads.* Pew Research Center. https://www.pewresearch.org/fact-tank/2019/06/12/fathers-day-facts/

Machin, A. (2021, June 19). *In praise of fathers: The making of the modern dad.* The Guardian. https://www.theguardian.com/lifeandstyle/2021/jun/19/in-praise-of-fathers-the-making-of-the-modern-dad

Marcin, A. (2020, April 14). *Pregnant and horny? Your pregnancy sex drive explained.* Healthline. https://www.healthline.com/health/pregnancy/pregnant-and-horny

Marcin, A. (2020, September 10). *Hospital bag checklist for mom and baby.* Healthline. https://www.healthline.com/health/pregnancy/hospital-bag-checklist

Marnach, M. (2021, December 7). *Ovulation signs: When is conception most likely?* Mayo Clinic. https://www.mayoclinic.org/healthy-lifestyle/getting-pregnant/expert-answers/ovulation-signs/faq-20058000

Marple, K. (2021, July 19). *4 weeks pregnant*. BabyCenter. https://www.babycenter.com/pregnancy/week-by-week/4-weeks-pregnant

MedlinePlus. (n.d). *Amniotic fluid*. https://medlineplus.gov/ency/article/002220.htm

Miles, K. (2021a). *Growth chart: Fetal length and weight, week by week*. BabyCenter. https://www.babycenter.com/pregnancy/your-body/growth-chart-fetal-length-and-weight-week-by-week_1290794

Miles, K. (2021b). *PUPPP rash during pregnancy*. BabyCenter https://www.babycenter.com/pregnancy/your-body/puppp-rash_40008036

Millard, E. (2021, October 12). *Constipation during pregnancy: How to get relief*. BabyCenter. https://www.babycenter.com/pregnancy/your-body/constipation-during-pregnancy_836

Murray, D. 2021. *How much calcium do you need during pregnancy?* Verywell Family. https://www.verywellfamily.com/calcium-needs-during-pregnancy-4580491

National Childbirth Trust. (2019, January 5). *Emotions during pregnancy*. https://www.nct.org.uk/pregnancy/how-you-might-be-feeling/emotions-during-pregnancy

NHS. (2019, May 1). *How can I tell when I'm ovulating?* https://www.nhs.uk/common-health-questions/womens-health/how-can-i-tell-when-i-am-ovulating/

O'Connor, A. (2021, September 27). *How can I tell the difference between Braxton Hicks contractions and labor contractions? What to Expect.* https://www.whattoexpect.com/pregnancy/symptoms -and-solutions/braxton-hicks-contractions.aspx

Olson, D., Sikka, R. S., Hayman, J., Novak, M. & Stavig, C. (2009). Exercise in pregnancy. *Current Sports Medicine Reports, 8*(3), 147–153. https://doi.org/10.1249/jsr.0b013e3181a61d51

Parker, K., Horowitz, J. M. & Stepler, R. (2017, December 5). *2. Americans see different expectations for men and women.* Pew Research Center. https://www.pewresearch.org/social-trends/2017/12/05/americans-see-different-expectations-for-men-and-women/#public-sees-more-pressure-for-men-on-job-and-career-front

Pearce, D. (n.d.). *A quote from Single Dad Laughing.* Good Reads. https://www.goodreads.com/quotes/1031122-the-greatest-mark-of-a-father-is-how-he-treats

Pearson, C. (2017). *7 awesome things your body does during pregnancy.* HuffPost. https://www.huffpost.com/entry/pregnancy-changes_n_3790822

Pediatric Associates of Franklin. (2018, August 7). *The importance of a father in a child's life.* https://www.pediatricsoffranklin.com/resources-and-education/pediatric-care/the-importance-of-a-father-in-a-childs-life/

Pevzner, H. (2021). *Week 16 of your pregnancy.* Verywell Family. https://www.verywellfamily.com/16-weeks-pregnant-4158998

Poblano, A., Haro, R. & Arteaga, C. (2008). Neurophysiologic measurement of continuity in the sleep of fetuses during the last week of pregnancy and in newborns. *International Journal of Biological Sciences*, 23–28. https://doi.org/10.7150/ijbs.4.23

Rhodes, A., Smith, A. D., Llewellyn, C. H., & Croker, H. (2021). Investigating partner involvement in pregnancy and identifying barriers and facilitators to participating as a couple in a digital healthy eating and physical activity intervention. *BMC Pregnancy and Childbirth, 21*(1). https://doi.org/10.1186/s12884-021-03917-z

Robinson, B. (2020, July 11). *Pregnancy discrimination in the workplace affects mother and baby health*. Forbes. https://www.forbes.com/sites/bryanrobinson/2020/07/11/pregnancy-discrimination-in-the-workplace-affects-mother-and-baby-health/

Rose, J. (2018). *Emily Blunt & John Krasinski's Parenting fears will make worried parents feel less alone*. Romper. https://www.romper.com/p/emily-blunt-john-krasinski-spoke-about-their-parenting-fears-theyre-really-relatable-8689476

Sangsawang, B. & Sangsawang, N. (2013). Stress urinary incontinence in pregnant women: a review of prevalence, pathophysiology, and treatment. *International Urogynecology Journal, 24*(6), 901–912. https://doi.org/10.1007/s00192-013-2061-7

Sauer, M. (2022, June 27). *27 weeks pregnant*. BabyCenter. https://www.babycenter.com/pregnancy/week-by-week/27-weeks-pregnant#pregnancy-symptoms

Scogna, K. 2021. *Your baby's umbilical cord*. BabyCenter. https://www.babycenter.com/pregnancy/your-baby/fetal-development-the-umbilical-cord_40007754

Showell, B. (2021, June 25). *Ovulation symptoms: 7 signs of ovulation.* The Bump. https://www.thebump.com/a/ovulation-symptoms-signs-of-ovulation

Suglia, C. (2017). *Magic Johnson's advice for parents of LGBT kids.* Romper. https://www.romper.com/p/magic-johnson-says-parents-of-lgbt-kids-need-to-show-support-because-they-may-not-get-it-elsewhere-52462

Tabackman, L. (2021, October 21). *Your first prenatal visit.* Healthline. https://www.healthline.com/health/pregnancy/evaluation-physician

Treasure Quotes. (n.d.). *Michael Bublé famous quote.* https://www.treasurequotes.com/quotes/fatherhood-is-the-greatest-thing-that-could

U.S. Consumer Product Safety Commission. (n.d.). *Crib safety tips.* https://www.cpsc.gov/safety-education/safety-guides/cribs/crib-safety-tips

Venuti, J. (2020, January 29). *39 weeks pregnant.* BabyCenter. https://www.babycenter.com/pregnancy/week-by-week/39-weeks-pregnant

Washington, D. (2006). *A hand to guide me.* Meredith Books.

Weiss, R. E. (2017, November 6). *Changes in the mother's body during pregnancy: Month by month.* Health Central. https://www.healthcentral.com/slideshow/changes-in-mothers-body-pregnancy-month-by-month

Made in the USA
Columbia, SC
22 October 2022